MASTERPIECES

A Celebration of Food and Art in Virginia

MASTERPIECES

A Celebration of Food and Art in Virginia

Terry Ward Libby
Food photographs Reneé Comet

VMFA

Virginia Museum of Fine Arts
The Council of VMFA
Richmond, Virginia

Library of Congress Cataloging-in-Publication Data available.

ISBN 0-917046-79-X

Printed in Verona, Italy by Mondadori

Published by Virginia Museum of Fine Arts and
The Council of VMFA, 200 N. Boulevard, Richmond,
Virginia 23220

Photographs for works on pages 11, 12, 13, 24, 65, 86,
    116, and 117 by VMFA Staff.
Photographs on pages 14 and 15 courtesy of the Virginia
    Department of Agriculture and Consumer Services.
Photograph on page 16 by Charles Shoffner.
All other VMFA works photographed by Katherine
    Wetzel.
Food styled by Lisa Cherkasky.

Edited by Ross Howell and Anne Adkins
Book Design by Carolyn Weary Brandt
Project Managed and Compiled by Sara Johnson-Ward
Composed by the designer in Adobe Pagemaker 7
Typeset in Adobe Garamond 3 and Futura
Printed on 150 gsm Gardamatte demi matte text

This book is underwritten
with generous support from
The Council of VMFA
in celebration of
their 50th anniversary.

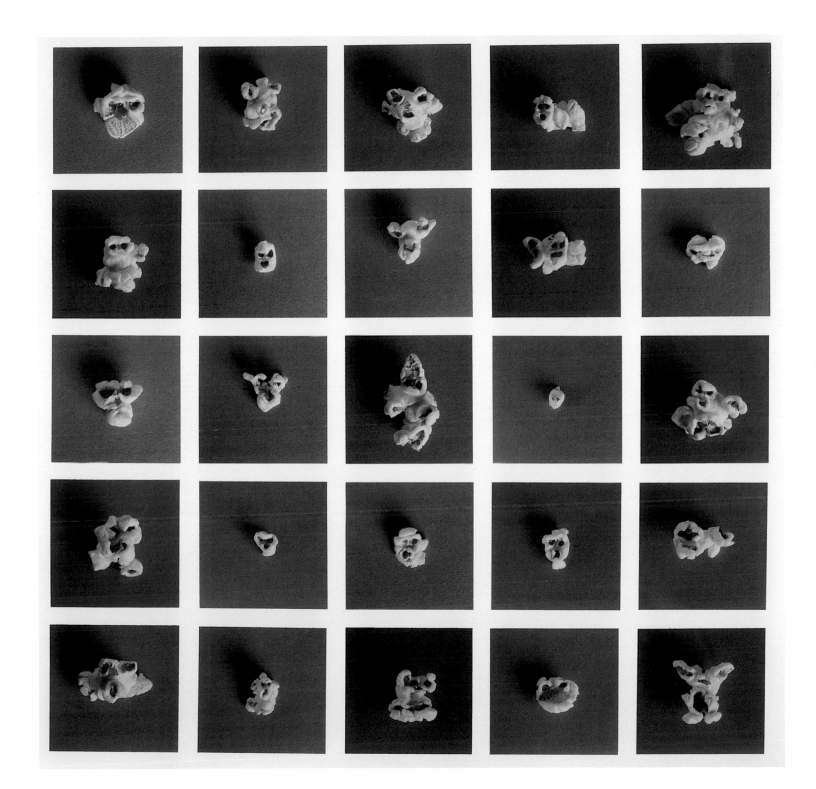

TABLE OF CONTENTS

ACKNOWLEDGMENTS

When this project began, its intent was to serve as a reminder of the strengths of the arts community around Virginia. To accomplish this, the Virginia Museum of Fine Arts and the Council decided to solicit recipes from its Statewide Curators' Roundtable. Twenty-two members participated by submitting recipes. As the project evolved over several years, we decided the Council's 50th Anniversary was the perfect occasion to launch *Masterpieces: A Celebration of Food and Art in Virginia*. Over the past half century, the Council has significantly and seamlessly impacted arts programming around Virginia through the monies it has raised for VMFA. This book has come together through the efforts of more than 100 volunteers and arts professionals working throughout the Commonwealth.

I would like to thank the following persons for gathering recipes to be submitted on behalf of their organizations: Nancy Newhard-Farrar, Alleghany Highlands Arts & Crafts Center; Michael Dowell, Artisans Center of Virginia; Bonnie Eisenman, Beth Ahabah Museum and Archives; Roddy Moore, Blue Ridge Institute and Museum, Ferrum College; Shannon Williams, Chrysler Museum of Art; Donna Parris, Danville Museum of Fine Arts and History; Barbara Rothermel, Daura Gallery, Lynchburg College; Mary Lou Hultgren, Hampton University Museum; Janet Ruth Carty, Hollins Art Gallery, Hollins University; Sandy Treanor, McLean Project for the Arts; Anne Hart and Judy Rauck, Peninsula Fine Arts Center; Toy Cobbe, Piedmont Arts Association; Steve Arbury, Radford University Art Museum; Leigh Anne Chambers, Rawls Museum Arts; Beth Cheuk, Thomas Jefferson Memorial Foundation; Trudi Van Dyke, Torpedo Factory Arts Center; Elizabeth Schlatter, University of Richmond Museums; Mike Alexander, University of Virginia Art Museum; Anna Fariello, Virginia Tech; Michelle Wilson, Tina Brand, David Bradley, Margaret Reynolds, Cathy Turner, and Aleksandra Totskiy, Virginia Museum of Fine Arts; Penny Lloyd, Virginia's Explore Park; and Betsy White, William King Regional Arts Center. The recipe authors are credited with the name of their organization on the page where their recipe appears. We thank each of them for sharing the pleasures of cookery from their kitchens with us.

Many, many volunteers tested recipes and helped to narrow the selection to what is presented in these pages. Their assistance was invaluable in creating the best cookbook possible. Our thanks extend to the following: Billy R. Allen, Jeffrey Allison, Anne Barriault, David Bradley, Deanna Brinkman, Jessica Browning, Susie Burtch, Carol Casstevens, Marjorie Claybrook, Valerie Coleman, Karen D. Daly, Meg Eastman, Jenny Evans, Suzanne Freeman, Wren Gillespie, Kathy Z. Gillis, Miffy Hall, Aiesha Halstead, Mary Holland, Matthew

Ipock, Lane Jackson, Carolyn and John Johnson, Mary Jo Kearfott, Alice McLeod, Carol Moon, Nancy Nichols, Trudy Norfleet, Karen Palen, Dawn Penny, Janet Ralston, Helen Redford, Margaret Reynolds, Jacky Robinson, Sandra Rogers, Sandy Rusak, Ruth Sancez, Lee Schultz, Rob Schultz, Mary Douglas Stanley, David Stover, Betty Thompson, Ruth Twiggs, Brent Ward, Della Watkins, Matthew Wiggins, Michelle Wilson, and Lulan Yu.

I am also grateful to VMFA staff and former staff members who performed the day-to-day tasks that accumulate to make a publication such as this. The following staff members have either provided the groundwork for reaching our art partners around Virginia, aided with organizing the materials for the book, assisted with photography needs, reviewed art historical information for accuracy, and/or provided guidance for aesthetic and sensory experience for the art and food featured: David McKinney, Eileen Mott, Sandy Rusak, David Pittman, the Collections and Research Committee, Michelle Wilson, Sarah Lavicka, Rosalie West, Suzanne Freeman, Kathy McDaniel, Aleksandra Totskiy, Lulan Yu, Candy Banks, Susie Rock, Lisa Hancock, Susan Turbeville, Kathy Morris, Howell Perkins, Katherine Wetzel, Randy Wilkinson, Geoff Strong, David Curry, Joseph Dye, Fred Brandt, Shawn Eichman, Tosha Grantham, Maggie Mayo, Beth O'Leary, John Ravenal, Cathy Turner, Barbara Lenhardt, and Michael Brand. Additional thanks go to Carol Amato and Ruth Twiggs for being enthusiastic, supportive, and willing to help in a pinch.

The refinement and charming presentation of the material would not have been possible without Ross Howell of Howell Press, Carolyn Brandt, Terry Ward Libby, Renée Comet, Lisa Cherkasky, Sabine Scherer, Anne Adkins, and generous donations by Mikasa and Crate and Barrel. Finally, this cookbook would not have stayed on schedule or presented itself so deliciously without the invaluable work of the cookbook committee members who are Council members: Betsy Stevenson, President; Wrenn Gillespie, First Vice President; and Margaret Reynolds, Development Chairman (all 2003-2005 term).

We all hope that every cook finds a recipe here that they like. We have included recipes that reflect old and new Virginia and that are designed for a beginning cook to a skilled chef. While preparing a dish from the cookbook, please enjoy the beautiful works of art that embellish the pages. Thank you for supporting the arts with the purchase of these delectable recipes. Bon Appetit!

Sara Johnson-Ward
Project Manager

FOREWORD

Fifty years ago, and just nineteen years after the Virginia Museum of Fine Arts was founded, the VMFA Board of Trustees invited forty-nine young women from Richmond to launch what was to become one of this institution's most vital groups. The Council of VMFA was formed with the goals of increasing membership, educating its members about the collections, furthering community interest in the Museum, and contributing to Museum programs through participation, sponsorship, and fundraising.

The Council has indeed supported the Museum in these and a great many other ways through the donation of their members' time and talents: funds raised by the group have occasionally been used to purchase works of art for the collection but more often have supported educational programs. The Council has organized numerous creative and exciting events that benefit both the community and the institution.

Over the past half-century, The Council's contributions have left an indelible mark on VMFA. During that time, The Council has contributed countless hours of volunteer service and more than $6,393,000 in direct financial support. Through the group's continuing innovation and dedication, I know that they will help to bring us to even higher levels of achievement as we complete the most ambitious expansion in the Museum's history. On behalf of VMFA, it is with great admiration that I extend my deepest appreciation to the enormous support provided by The Council through its brilliant community leadership.

Dr. Michael Brand
Director

1955   The Council of VMFA, an all-volunteer support group, was started by 49 charter members.

1956   The Council held its first fundraiser, a *Fashion Festival of Arts and Flowers*.

1957   The Loan-Own Gallery began, focusing on Virginia artists.

1959   The first annual *Viennese Ball* was held by The Council.

1960   The Council held its first annual *Holiday Open House*, which continues today.

1962   The Council opened the Museum Shop with proceeds supporting VMFA programs.

      Seventy four Council volunteers signed up to work in the VMFA library.

1963   Members of The Council began training and serving as gallery tour guides.

      The Council began its support of the VMFA library and continues its support today.

1965   An evening event, *Unwinder* began. Today VMFA sponsors a similar event, *Art after Hours*.

1968	The Council Curator Fund was started and the first *Corporate Patrons Gala* was hosted.
1973	The Travel Committee was formed, organizing trips for VMFA members.
1974	Publication of *The Gallery Guide to the Virginia Museum* was funded by The Council.
1976	The Council held its first *Heirloom Discovery Day*.
1978	The Trustee-Council Contribution Fund was created.
1979	The Council supported the new Institute of Contemporary Art.
1980	The Council collaborated with the Junior League of Richmond on the Youth Gallery project.

	The Council celebrated its 25th Anniversary with a large financial contribution and gifts of art to VMFA.
1981	Ongoing support included VMFA's 45th Anniversary.
1984	The Speakers Bureau was started.
1985	*West Wing Gala* was hosted by The Council to raise money for the new structure.
	Hirschler Flower Endowment was established, ensuring that fresh cut flowers would grace the entrance to the VMFA Shop. Council members are responsible for the flower arrangements.
	Children's Saturday Workshops were funded and staffed by The Council.
	The Council gave seed money to start Friends of Art.
1987	The Council organized and hosted the first *Fine Arts & Flowers*.
1988	The Council collaborated with Youth and Family Programs to aid the Education and Outreach Departments.
1989	The Council hosted the opening gala for the exhibition, *Romance of the Taj Mahal*.
	The Council organized and hosted *Fine Arts & Flowers 1989*.

1990	A grant from The Council gave 55 professional development awards to 22 Statewide Affiliates.
1991	The Council numbered 1,022 members who gave more than 45,000 hours of service per year.
1992	The Council produced the cookbook, *Virginia Celebrates*, with proceeds donated to Education and Outreach efforts.
1993	Proceeds from *Fine Arts & Flowers 1993* supported the exhibition, *The Making of Virginia Architecture*.
1994	The Council sponsored *Sotheby's Heirloom Discovery Day* on November 5, 1994.
1995	The Council celebrated its 40th anniversary with a gift to VMFA. *Fine Arts & Flowers 1995* was held with proceeds supporting VMFA.
1997	Proceeds from *Fine Arts & Flowers 1997* went toward landscaping for the renovation of the Center for Education and Outreach.
1998	The Council sponsored the sold-out event, *Women of Style and Substance*.
1999	The Council sponsored a special gala, *Night on the Nile*, to celebrate the opening of the exhibition, *Egypt*.
2000	The Council made a Millennium Gift to VMFA, establishing the Council Endowment for Educational Programs. The grand total of all Council support to VMFA was $935,494. *Fine Arts & Flowers 2000* was celebrated. Active Council volunteers provided 50,183 hours of service.
2001	The Council joined with Friends of Art to host the opening gala, *Night Nouveau*. The gala commemorated the exhibition, *Celebrating Art Nouveau: The Kruezer Collection*.
2002	The Council completed a Strategic Business Plan governing its structure and operations for the future.
2003	*Fine Arts & Flowers 2003* was held.
2004	The Council made plans for a new shop to open in the West Wing galleries during VMFA's expansion.
2005	The Council supported the publication of the cookbook, *Masterpieces: A Celebration of Food and Art in Virginia* and commemorated its 50th Anniversary.

The Museum's primary objective is to contribute to the education and the pleasure of the people of Virginia and the Council's aim will be to further that objective.

—Mrs. E. Angus Powell,
Head of the Council
May 17, 1955

INTRODUCTION

It is a truism that art imitates nature.

Virginia, America's first farm state, offers a giant canvas upon which we can color a vast array of agricultural products to be used for our enjoyment.

If I were an artist, I would paint our Commonwealth in different hues of verdant green with meandering rivers teeming with fish. Using a primitive style, I would make brush strokes that convey grasslands with grazing farm animals, meadows with cultivated plots of vegetables, and orchards with fruit trees in full bloom. Nearby vineyards would show vines heavy with wine-grape clusters awaiting harvest.

My painting would reflect that we are principally an agricultural state, with farms situated on 34 percent of Virginia's total acreage. Almost anything can be grown somewhere in our state, taking into consideration climatic conditions. It is no wonder that we have such a rich tradition of foods and culinary adventures.

Generations of farm families continue to grow the produce of their ancestors. It is not difficult to find farmers whose families have been operating their sites for at least one hundred years. Their efforts, coupled with newcomers introducing items never before produced in the state, add to our cornucopia of regional foods.

14

The earliest English colonists arriving in Virginia in the 1600s learned how to hunt and fish and farm important crops from the existing Indian tribes. Many of the foods that we eat today can be traced back to the influence of these Native Americans, who taught the settlers the basics of cultivating native plants. Recipes from those Colonial days and the Southern cooks of the great plantations still enrich our culinary heritage.

The most famous gardener of Virginia's early agricultural history was Thomas Jefferson, who also has the distinction of being called "the father of American wine." Growing many varieties of wine grapes on his hillside vineyard, Jefferson's experiments 200 years ago with more than seventy varieties of vegetables, rare fruits, and horticultural plantings are admired by gardeners the world over.

We are fortunate to live in Virginia, where 50,000 farms flourish and where fish are so readily available in our fresh and salt waters. Our waters teem with fifty commercial seafood species. Different climatic conditions in our farming regions provide fertile soil for almost any crop to grow.

The bounty of diverse agriculture includes fruits, grains, vegetables, and peanuts. Beef and dairy cattle as well as pork and lamb abound, along with chickens, turkeys, and game fowl.

New entries in the food field are leaner meats from bison and Piedmontese beef; ostriches and emus are

being bred for the same purpose. These meats are gaining a reputation with Virginia chefs seeking to provide healthier meals for their customers.

Some farmers are catering to a more sophisticated cuisine by growing tasty mushroom varieties, soy beans, year-round hydroponic tomatoes, and hothouse herbs and salad greens. These are obtainable at in-season local farmers' markets in the cities and at fruit and vegetable stands in the country. There are growers who offer "pick your own" berries, apples, and melons in their gardens. The aim of these projects is to bring the best and the freshest produce directly to the consumer.

Virginians have been known for years for their successful agricultural pursuits. But one, the cultivation of wine grapes that would make a palate-pleasing wine, has eluded them for 400 years—that is, until our present generation pioneered in vineyard plantings and the 1970s Farm Winery Act was established.

We have the oldest wine-growing history of the original thirteen English colonies. Efforts to grow wine grapes from native varieties failed because the vines could not survive weather conditions, or if they did, their fruit made unpalatable wine. Native Scuppernong grapes were among the earliest varieties grown in the Tidewater area, but because the wine was inferior, vineyards proved unprofitable.

Thomas Jefferson's efforts at Monticello to grow European grapes that produced his favorite wines were a lifelong experiment. He believed in the virtues of wines and thought that grape-growing would make a fine crop for his fellow Virginians. Sadly, the vines were not suited to his vineyard site and no wine was produced from any of his plantings. Yet Jefferson remains as the inspiration for wine-grape growing of this era.

It was not until the 1970s that viticulture in Virginia had advanced enough to enable early farm winery pioneers to grow French-American hybrid grape varieties that produced pleasant wines. The goal, however, was to cultivate European vinifera grapes. This was accomplished later. Excellent wines from Riesling,

Chardonnay, and Cabernet Sauvignon grapes were finally produced—after the struggles of 400 years—thanks to viticultural and enological research. This success has encouraged others. In 1976 there were five wineries in Virginia; today, there are eighty-five. Each year more wineries are being licensed. And the state has shown unprecedented support for this new agricultural industry. It has been a boon to winegrowers that our present governor, Mark Warner, has a successful vineyard at his home in King George, Virginia.

Tasting rooms are now meccas for thousands of tourists seeking to sample the highly touted wines of Virginia. Because of our scenic beauty and historic past, we can offer visitors an experience in wine touring that is unlike any other wine-growing region in the East. Established wineries are found across the Commonwealth, from the Eastern Shore to the Southwest Highlands.

With the plethora of Virginia foods available, wineries are growing grape varieties suited to pairing with every imaginable menu. And medals from national and international competitions are proof that Virginia wines compete well with wines from all other parts of the world.

The most popular white grapes grown in Virginia are European varietal counterparts of Chardonnay, Riesling, Pinot Grigio, and Viognier. The reds are Merlot, Cabernet Sauvignon, and Cabernet Franc. French-American hybrid white grapes like Seyval Blanc and Vidal Blanc and the red Chambourcin have found a niche among less experienced wine drinkers when they are vinified leaving some residual sugar. Their fruitiness pleases individuals who dislike dry wines but enjoy a tamer version of barrel-aged viniferas.

At the other end of the spectrum, sophisticated palates are celebrating with medal-winning Virginia sparkling wines made in true *Méthode Champenoise*. We are also producing late-harvest wines that rival the lovely dessert wines from Europe's well-known wine regions.

Wine and food are best served together, with the flavors of each complementing the other. Today's home cooks have the extraordinary opportunity to test their culinary skills with recipes pairing wines and foods. There are step-by-step instructions in newspapers, magazines, television cooking shows, and on the Worldwide Web. Never before in our history have we had the opportunity to learn more about what we eat and drink and how best to combine them. The best wines and finest foods are now grown here in Virginia.

With this bounty, home cooks across Virginia have the opportunity to present a culinary triumph with an exciting choice of wine, a combination as exquisite as an artist's work of art.

Felicia Rogan
Owner of Oakencroft Vineyard and Winery
Former VMFA Trustee

17

CHAPTER 1
APPETIZERS

Artichoke Hearts Sautéed
with Serrano Ham

Serves 4.

1 pound artichoke hearts (see recipe note)
2 tablespoons olive oil
1/4 cup finely diced Serrano ham
2 cloves of garlic, thinly sliced
1/4 teaspoon freshly ground pepper
2 tablespoons minced fresh parsley

1. Prepare the artichoke hearts. Heat the olive oil in a large skillet. Add the artichoke hearts, ham, garlic, and pepper. Sautè the mixture for 10 minutes over medium heat.

2. Pour the hot mixture into a serving bowl and sprinkle with parsley. Serve with crusty French bread.

Recipe Note
You may prepare fresh artichoke hearts for this recipe, or use frozen artichoke hearts prepared according to package directions. Canned, water-packed artichoke hearts may also be used. It is important that they are well-drained and lightly towel-dried before use.

Suzanne Freeman
Head Librarian and Publications Manager
VMFA, Richmond

Boursin Cheese Spread

Makes 1/2 cup.

8 ounces cream cheese at room temperature
1 teaspoon dried basil
1 teaspoon dried oregano
1 teaspoon dried thyme
1 teaspoon crushed garlic

Cream all the ingredients together until smooth.
Cover and refrigerate until ready to use.
Serve with crackers or slices of crusty bread.

Linda Blake, Gallery Manager
Artisans Center of Virginia, Waynesboro

Eggplant Caponata

Serves 4.

¼ cup olive oil

1 medium eggplant, unpeeled, cut into 1-inch cubes

1 medium onion, diced

1 stalk celery, diced

1 large clove garlic, minced

1 (16-ounce) can diced tomatoes, with juice

1½ teaspoons dried basil

2 teaspoons dried oregano

½ cup chopped black or green olives

2 tablespoons capers, drained

2 tablespoons balsamic vinegar, or more to taste

1½ teaspoons granulated sugar

¼ cup dry red wine

Salt and pepper to taste

1. Heat the olive oil in a large skillet or Dutch oven. Add the eggplant and sauté until light, golden brown. Add onion, celery and garlic, and sauté 5 minutes more.

2. Add tomatoes, basil, and oregano and simmer, uncovered, for 15 minutes. Add the olives, capers, vinegar, sugar, and wine. Continue to simmer for 15 to 20 minutes, stirring occasionally, until the vegetables are tender and the mixture has thickened. Season to taste with salt and pepper.

3. Allow the Caponata to cool, then transfer it to the bowl of food processor. Pulse once or twice, just until the vegetables are coarsely diced. Serve at room temperature on slices of toasted French bread spread with Boursin (see recipe on previous page).

VARIATION

For a main course, toss warm Eggplant Caponata, 8 ounces of hot cooked pasta, and 4 ounces of crumbled goat cheese in a large pasta bowl. Serve topped with shredded Romano or Parmigiano cheese. Serves 2.

Linda Blake, Gallery Manager
Artisans Center of Virginia, Waynesboro

This is a wonderful appetizer and also makes a fantastic main course when served over hot pasta.

Fritters of Bitto Cheese in Truffle Batter

**Serves 4 as an appetizer;
8 to 10 as canapés.**

Buckwheat flour and Bitto cheese are commonly used in the kitchens of Valtellina, in the Lombardy region of Italy. The flour is widely available in the U.S., but the cheese may prove more difficult to find. Bitto is made from raw cow's milk combined with a small percentage of goat's milk. Like Parmigiano-Reggiano, it is aged in large wheels for many months. If you cannot locate this specific cheese, look for a high-quality Gruyère or Fontina. Many truffle products are available in specialty grocery stores, though fresh white truffles are rare and very expensive. Look for a small jar of truffle paste or truffle-infused oil to use instead.

The fritters may be served atop dressed salad greens as an appetizer, or served alone from a tray as party canapés.

1½ cups buckwheat flour
¾ cup all-purpose flour
2 teaspoons salt
2 ounces grappa, or other clear liquor, such as
   vodka
2 to 3 cups sparkling mineral water, such as
   San Pellegrino Frizzante
1 ounce chopped fresh white truffles (substitute
   2 tablespoons truffle paste or truffle-infused oil)
8 ounces Bitto cheese, cut into ½-inch cubes
Vegetable oil for deep-frying
4 cups baby lettuce greens
4 tablespoons extra-virgin olive oil
2 tablespoons aged balsamic vinegar, or more
   to taste

1. In a large mixing bowl, toss the flours and salt together with a spatula. Whisk in the grappa (or other liquor) and enough sparkling water until the mixture resembles pancake batter. Stir in the truffle product. Refrigerate the batter for at least 30 minutes.

2. Heat the oil to 325°F in a deep, heavy pot or portable frying machine. Place the cheese cubes in the batter and coat completely. Using tongs or a slotted spoon, lift the cheese cubes from the batter and carefully drop them into the hot oil, one at a time. Do not overcrowd the pot or the fritters may burst. When the fritters are golden brown, about 3 to 5 minutes, remove them from the oil and drain on paper towels.

3. Divide the baby lettuce greens among 4 appetizer or salad plates, drizzle with the olive oil and balsamic vinegar, then top with the warm Bitto fritters.

**Melissa Close, Chef
Palladio Restaurant
Barboursville Vineyards, Barboursville
Courtesy VMFA, Richmond**

Mushrooms in Garlic Sauce

Serves 4.

Serve this appetizer with a
crusty bread for dipping
into the delicious pan juices.

3 tablespoons extra-virgin olive oil

8 ounces fresh mushrooms, trimmed, brushed clean,
   and sliced

4 cloves garlic, peeled and thinly sliced

2 teaspoons fresh lemon juice

2 tablespoons dry Spanish sherry

1/4 cup beef broth

1/2 teaspoon sweet paprika

1/2 dried small red chile pepper, seeded and crumbled,
   or 1/4 teaspoon crushed red pepper flakes

Salt and freshly ground pepper to taste

1 tablespoon minced fresh parsley for garnish

1. Heat the olive oil in a skillet until very hot. Add
the mushrooms and garlic and sauté over high heat for
about 2 minutes, or until the mushrooms release their
liquid and begin to brown. Lower heat and stir in the
lemon juice, sherry, broth, paprika, and chile pepper.

2. Simmer 2 minutes more, then season to taste with
salt and pepper. Sprinkle with parsley before serving.

Suzanne Freeman
**Head Librarian and Publications Manager
VMFA, Richmond**

24

Hampton Roads Crab Cakes

Serves 4 as an appetizer;
2 as an entrée.

This recipe will yield 16 small canapé-sized crab cakes, or 4 generous crab cakes that can be served as entrées to serve 2.

Crab Cake Mixture

1 pound backfin crabmeat, picked over for any
   shell bits

8 saltine crackers, finely crushed

1 egg, lightly beaten

1 tablespoon prepared yellow mustard

1 tablespoon mayonnaise

1 teaspoon Old Bay seasoning

1 tablespoon chopped fresh parsley

Salt and pepper to taste

$\frac{1}{4}$ cup ($\frac{1}{2}$ stick) butter for frying

1. Gently fold together all the ingredients for the crab cake mixture.

2. Heat the butter in a heavy frying pan. To make canapé-sized crab cakes, shape the mixture into 16 bite-size cakes and sauté over medium-high heat, turning once, until golden on both sides.

3. To make entrée-sized crab cakes, divide the mixture into four patties and sauté as described above.

Anne Hart, Volunteer
Peninsula Fine Arts Center
Newport News

Crab and Cheese Bites

Serves 6 to 8.

¼ cup (½ stick) butter at room temperature

1 (5-ounce) jar Kraft Old English pasteurized
  cheese spread

2 tablespoons mayonnaise

½ pound fresh crabmeat, picked over for any shell
  bits

4 English muffins, split

1. In the bowl of a food processor combine the butter, Old English cheese spread, mayonnaise, and crabmeat until nearly smooth. Spread the muffin halves with the mixture, place on a baking sheet, cover with plastic wrap, and place in the freezer for at least 30 minutes, or until ready to prepare.

2. Preheat the broiler. Broil the muffins until bubbly and lightly browned, 5 to 7 minutes. Serve hot, with each muffin-half cut into quarters.

Virginia Holton
Former First Lady of Virginia
Courtesy McLean Project for the Arts

Crabmeat with Dill on Cayenne Toasts

Makes 24 canapés.

For the Toasts
6 slices firm white sandwich bread

3 tablespoons unsalted butter

$\frac{1}{8}$ teaspoon cayenne pepper

$\frac{1}{4}$ teaspoon salt

For the Crabmeat Spread
1 tablespoon minced shallots

1 tablespoon chopped fresh dill, plus several sprigs for garnish

2 tablespoons mayonnaise

2 tablespoons sour cream

2 teaspoons fresh lemon juice

Salt to taste

6 ounces jumbo lump crabmeat, picked over for any shell bits

1. Preheat oven to 350°F. To make the toasts, stack the bread slices and, using a sharp, serrated bread knife, trim off the crusts. Quarter the slices to make twenty-four $1\frac{1}{2}$-inch squares. Arrange the squares on a baking sheet.

2. In a small sauce pan, melt the butter and stir in the cayenne and salt. Brush the tops of the squares with the butter mixture and bake on a middle rack in the oven until pale golden, about 10 minutes. Cool the toasts on a rack. These may be made a day ahead and kept in an airtight container at room temperature.

3. In a bowl, blend together the shallots, dill, mayonnaise, sour cream and lemon juice. Salt the mixture to taste, then gently fold in the crabmeat. Cover and chill thoroughly before serving.

4. To serve, mound about $\frac{1}{2}$ tablespoon crabmeat spread on each toast and garnish with a small sprig of dill.

Judy Rauch, Volunteer
Peninsula Fine Arts Center, Newport News

Shrimp in Garlic Sauce

Serves 4.

1 pound small to medium-sized raw shrimp, peeled
    and deveined
Coarse salt
½ cup extra-virgin olive oil
1 tablespoon minced fresh garlic
1 dried small red chile pepper, seeded and
    crumbled, or ¼ teaspoon crushed red pepper
    flakes
1 tablespoon minced fresh parsley

1. Dry the shrimp well on paper towels, then
sprinkle with salt on both sides. Let rest at room
temperature for 10 minutes before frying.

2. Heat the olive oil in a shallow frying pan. Add
the garlic and chile pepper, and sauté over medium-
high heat until the garlic is lightly golden, about 1
to 2 minutes.

3. Working quickly, add the shrimp and sauté for
about 2 minutes more, or until the shrimp are just
done (opaque and heated through). Remove the pan
from the heat and pour the shrimp and the pan liquids into a serving bowl. Sprinkle with the parsley
and add salt to taste, if needed. Serve immediately
and provide lots of good bread for dunking.

Suzanne Freeman
Head Librarian and Publications Manager
VMFA, Richmond

Ghent Shrimp

Serves 8 to 10.

The shrimp in this tangy marinade can be eaten alone as an hors d'oeuvre, or served over a bed of mesclun greens and chilled pasta.

Marinade
¾ cup Dijon mustard
¾ cup canola oil
4 tablespoons ketchup
½ cup white wine vinegar
1 red bell pepper, seeded and minced
1 green bell pepper, seeded and minced
3 scallions (green onions), chopped
Tabasco sauce to taste
Salt and pepper to taste

2 to 3 pounds cooked fresh shrimp, peeled and
    deveined

1. Whisk together all the marinade ingredients in a
bowl large enough to hold all the shrimp. Add the
shrimp and toss with the marinade, coating well.

2. Cover and chill the shrimp in the marinade for
at least 2 hours before serving.

Katherine Bingham, Representative
Freemason Street Reception Center
Chrysler Museum of Art, Norfolk

Pork and Crabmeat Balls with Hot Apricot Mustard Dip

Makes approximately 80 bite-sized meatballs.

For the Meatballs

2 tablespoons butter

1 red bell pepper, seeded and finely diced

½ medium red onion, finely diced (about ¾ cup)

2 scallions (green onions), finely chopped

5 pounds ground pork

2 pounds backfin crabmeat, picked over for any shell bits

3 tablespoons siracha sauce (Asian red chile paste)

3 tablespoons fresh chopped cilantro

1 teaspoon Thai fish sauce

2 tablespoons chopped fresh garlic

2 tablespoons ground ginger

1 teaspoon salt

½ teaspoon freshly ground black pepper

For the Hot Apricot Mustard Dip

2 tablespoons mirin (Japanese rice wine for cooking)

1 (12-ounce) jar apricot jelly

Dry mustard to taste

1. Melt the butter in a skillet and add the red bell pepper, red onion, and scallions (green onions). Sauté over medium-high heat until the vegetables are just soft, about 5 to 7 minutes. Remove the mixture to a large mixing bowl and allow it to cool to room temperature.

2. Add the remaining meatball ingredients and combine well, using your hands or an electric mixer.

3. Preheat the oven to 350°F. Roll the mixture into 1-inch balls and space them at least an inch apart on a cookie sheet. Bake for 15 minutes, until cooked through.

4. While the meatballs are baking, whisk the mirin with the apricot jelly until smooth. Whisk in dry mustard by teaspoonfuls to achieve the desired degree of "heat"—the more mustard, the hotter the dip will be.

5. Serve the meatballs hot from the oven on a platter, with Hot Apricot Mustard Dip on the side.

Danny Ayers, Executive Chef
VMFA, Richmond

31

Water Chestnut Meatballs

**Makes approximately
40 to 50 meatballs.**

This recipe is equally good as
an hors d'oeuvre for a crowd or
as an entrée, served
with steamed rice.

2 cups soft (fresh) bread crumbs

$1/2$ cup whole milk

1 tablespoon soy sauce

1 clove minced fresh garlic

$1/4$ cup grated onion

$1/2$ teaspoon salt

$1/2$ pound ground beef

$1/2$ pound ground pork

1 (5-ounce) can water chestnuts, drained and finely
   chopped

1 jar Chinese plum sauce for dipping

1. Preheat oven to 350°F. Combine bread crumbs, milk, soy sauce, garlic, onion, and salt in large mixing bowl.

2. Add the ground beef, ground pork, and water chestnuts. Mix the ingredients well, using your hands or an electric mixer.

3. Roll the mixture into 1-inch balls and space them at least an inch apart on a cookie sheet. Bake at 350°F for 18 to 20 minutes, until cooked through.

VARIATION

For a "quick" version of this recipe, $1/2$ teaspoon garlic powder and $1/2$ teaspoon onion salt can be substituted for the fresh garlic, onion, and salt above.

Barbara Rothermel, Director
Daura Gallery/Museum Studies Program
Lynchburg College

CHAPTER 2

BREAKFAST AND BRUNCH

Monticello Muffins, or Griddle Cakes

Makes 24 small muffins.

The "Receipt for Monticello Muffins" was recorded in the manuscript cookbook of Thomas Jefferson's granddaughter Septimia Randolph Meikleham:

"To a quart of flour put two table spoonsfull of yeast. Mix the flour up with water so thin that the dough will stick to the table. Our cook takes it up and throws it down until it will no longer stick. She puts it to rise until morning. In the morning she works the dough over the first thing and makes it into little cakes like biscuit and sets them aside until it is time to bake them. You know muffins are baked in a griddle in the hearth of the stove not inside. They bake very quickly. The second plate full is put on the fire when breakfast is sent in and they are ready by the time the first are eaten."

Here is an adaptation of this original recipe by Monticello staff members Susan McCrary and Katherine G. Revell. The muffins are best cooked on a cast iron griddle or in a heavy skillet.

4 cups all-purpose flour, plus additional for
    kneading
1 1/2 packets (3 1/2 teaspoons) active dry yeast
1 1/2 cups water

1. In a large mixing bowl, blend the flour, yeast, and water. The dough will be very sticky.

2. Coat your hands with flour, then turn the dough out onto a flat, floured surface. Knead the dough while adding small amounts of flour (up to 1/2 cup), until the dough loses its stickiness and pulls easily off the work surface.

3. Place the dough in a large bowl, cover with a towel, and leave in a warm place overnight. The dough should more than double by morning.

4. One hour before cooking the muffins, punch down the dough, knead it for 3 to 5 minutes, then roll it into 1 1/2-inch balls for the muffins. Cover again with a towel, and let the muffins rise for an additional hour.

5. Preheat an ungreased griddle or iron skillet over medium heat. Place the muffins on the griddle and cook for about 5 minutes on each side, until lightly browned. The muffins will look like biscuits on the outside, and English muffins on the inside. Serve hot.

Thomas Jefferson Memorial Foundation
Charlottesville

Pumpkin Ham Biscuits

**Makes 3 dozen
cocktail-sized biscuits,
or 1 dozen large biscuits.**

Stuff these warm biscuits with slices of sweet Virginia country ham or traditional Smithfield ham, a delicious salt-cured ham made in Virginia for generations.

In the VMFA Dining Room,
these biscuits are served alongside
a cool, crisp
shrimp salad.

5 cups all-purpose flour
1 tablespoon baking powder
$1/4$ teaspoon salt
1 tablespoon granulated sugar
1 cup cold butter, cut into small pieces
1 cup pumpkin purée
$1/4$ cup half-and-half
1 pound shaved ham

1. Preheat the oven to 350°F. Place the flour, baking powder, salt, and sugar in a large mixing bowl and toss with a spatula to combine.

2. Using a fork or pastry blender, cut in the butter a few pieces at a time, until the mixture resembles a coarse meal. Fold in the pumpkin purée, then the half-and-half, using just a few strokes to combine the biscuit dough—do not over-mix.

3. Dust a smooth work surface or pastry board with a small amount of flour. Place the dough on the surface and roll it to about $1/4$-inch thickness. For cocktail-sized biscuits use a 1-inch round cutter; for large biscuits, use a 3-inch round cutter.

4. Place the biscuits on a greased baking sheet. Bake 12 to 15 minutes for cocktail-sized biscuits; 18 to 20 minutes for large biscuits.

5. Remove the baking sheet from the oven, leaving the biscuits on the sheet until cool enough to handle. Split the warm biscuits, and fill each with thin slices of ham.

Stephanie Dungee, Baker
VMFA, Richmond

38

Louisiana Sausage Savory Coffee Cake

Makes 9 slices.

For the Filling
1 pound "hot" bulk sausage
$\frac{1}{2}$ cup chopped scallions (green onions)
$\frac{1}{4}$ cup grated Parmesan cheese
$\frac{1}{2}$ cup grated Swiss cheese
1 egg, lightly beaten
$\frac{1}{4}$ teaspoon Tabasco sauce, or more to taste
$\frac{1}{2}$ teaspoon salt
2 tablespoons chopped fresh parsley

For the Batter
2 cups Bisquick brand biscuit mix
$\frac{3}{4}$ cup whole milk
$\frac{1}{4}$ cup mayonnaise

For the Egg wash
1 egg yolk
1 tablespoon water

1. For the filling, crumble the sausage into a skillet, add the scallions (green onions), and brown together over medium heat, about 10 minutes. Drain off excess fat, transfer the mixture to a mixing bowl, and allow it to cool slightly. Fold in the cheeses, the beaten egg, Tabasco, salt, and parsley.

2. Preheat the oven to 350°F. Lightly grease a 9x9x2-inch baking pan. In a separate bowl, beat together the Bisquick, milk, and mayonnaise to make a thick batter. Spread half of the batter in the baking dish, then cover with the sausage mixture. Drop the remaining batter over the sausage by spoonfuls, then smooth the top with a spatula to cover the sausage mixture.

3. Make an egg wash by whisking together the egg yolk and water, then brush the wash over the batter, coating thoroughly. Bake for 25 to 30 minutes, or until the edges of the cake begin to pull away from the sides of the pan, and a wooden pick inserted near the center of the cake comes out clean.

4. Cool the cake 5 minutes before cutting into 3-inch squares.

VARIATION
For a spicier version, use crumbled andouille or chorizo sausage. This recipe can be doubled and baked in a 13x9x2-inch pan. The cake can also be sliced into 1-inch squares for canapé-sized portions.

Alma Powell
Courtesy McLean Project for the Arts

Cranberry-Apple Casserole

Serves 6 to 8.

This is a sweet, cobbler-like "casserole" to include in a brunch buffet. It is equally delicious as a dessert, served warm, along with a generous scoop of vanilla ice cream.

2 cups fresh or dried cranberries

3 cups peeled and diced baking apples, such as Granny Smiths

1 1/2 cups granulated sugar

For the Topping

1/2 cup (1 stick) butter at room temperature

1/2 cup brown sugar

1 cup "quick-cooking" oats

1/2 cup all-purpose flour

1/2 cup chopped pecans (or walnuts)

1. Preheat the oven to 350°F and lightly grease a 9x9x2-inch baking pan.

2. In a mixing bowl, toss together the cranberries, apples, and sugar. Press the fruit mixture into the baking pan.

3. Blend together the soft butter, brown sugar, oats, flour, and nuts until smooth. Spread the topping over the fruit. Bake for 1 hour, or until golden brown. Cool 15 minutes before cutting into squares.

Ann Drewry
Chair of Education and Outreach Committee
Alleghany Highlands Arts & Crafts Center
Clifton Forge

Chicken Asparagus Strata

Serves 6.

If you prepare diced chicken for this recipe by poaching a whole fryer, you will produce a pint or more of rich chicken stock, plus additional cooked chicken, that can be stored in the freezer for another use. An acceptable shortcut would be to poach one whole boneless, skinless chicken breast, diced to yield 3 cups.

This strata is assembled the day before it is to be baked and served.

For 3 cups Diced Chicken

1 whole (4-pound) frying chicken
2 cups water
1 small onion, sliced (about 1 cup)
3 celery tops with leaves
1 teaspoon salt
$^1/_4$ teaspoon pepper

For the Strata

$^1/_2$ cup mayonnaise
$^1/_3$ cup chopped onion
$^1/_3$ cup chopped celery
1 tablespoon lemon juice
$^1/_2$ teaspoon salt
$^1/_4$ teaspoon freshly ground black pepper
1 teaspoon Bell's poultry seasoning
8 slices whole wheat bread (crusts removed, cubed)

1 pound fresh asparagus spears, trimmed and cut into 1-inch lengths
4 eggs
3 cups whole milk
1 cup grated sharp Cheddar cheese

1. To poach a whole chicken, place the chicken, water, onion, celery tops, salt, and pepper in a stock pot just large enough to hold the chicken. Cover and simmer approximately 45 minutes, or until a fork can be inserted into the chicken with ease. Allow the chicken to cool in the stock, then pull the meat from the bones, discarding skin and any bits of cartilage. Strain the chicken stock, cover, and refrigerate or freeze. Alternately, to poach a whole boneless, skinless chicken breast (about 1 pound), simmer it in lightly salted water for approximately 20 minutes, then cool and dice.

2. In a mixing bowl, toss the diced chicken with the mayonnaise, chopped onion, celery, lemon juice, salt, pepper, and poultry seasoning.

3. Grease a 13x9x2-inch baking dish. Layer half the bread cubes in the dish, then spread the chicken mixture over the bread. Distribute the asparagus and remaining bread cubes over the chicken mixture.

4. In a separate bowl, beat the eggs and milk together. Pour evenly over the strata. Cover with plastic wrap and refrigerate for at least 4 hours or overnight.

5. To bake the strata, preheat the oven to 325°F. Bake the strata for 15 minutes, then remove from the oven and sprinkle with cheese. Bake for an additional 50 minutes, or until firm and lightly golden.

Doris T. Jones, Public Relations Manager
Danville Museum of Fine Arts and History

Pineapple-Cheese Bake

Serves 6 to 8.

1 (20-ounce) can pineapple chunks, drained, reserving 3 tablespoons can juices
1 cup shredded mild Cheddar cheese
1/2 cup granulated sugar
3 tablespoons all-purpose flour
1 cup crushed Ritz brand crackers
1/4 cup melted butter

1. Preheat the oven to 350°F and lightly grease a 1 1/2-quart baking pan or casserole dish.

2. In a mixing bowl, combine the pineapple chunks, reserved juice, cheese, sugar, and flour. Transfer the mixture to the prepared baking dish.

3. Combine the crushed crackers with the melted butter and sprinkle evenly over the pineapple mixture. Bake for 30 minutes, or until bubbly and golden.

Kim Brown, Assistant to the Director
William King Regional Arts Center, Abingdon

Frittata Anna

Serves 4 to 6.

4 tablespoons olive oil

1 medium onion, chopped (about 1 cup)

½ red bell pepper, seeded and chopped

8 eggs

1 pound fresh spinach, cooked and thoroughly
    drained

¼ teaspoon salt

¼ teaspoon freshly ground pepper

½ cup canned black olives, drained and cut in half

½ cup water-packed artichoke hearts, drained and
    coarsely chopped

½ cup chopped cooked bacon

2 tablespoons finely chopped fresh basil leaves

¼ cup shredded Parmesan cheese

1. In a large, oven-proof skillet, heat 2 tablespoons of the olive oil. Sauté the onion and bell pepper until soft, then remove the vegetables from the skillet and set aside.

2. In a mixing bowl, beat the eggs well, then fold in the cooked spinach, the sautéed onion and bell pepper mixture, salt, and pepper. Preheat the broiler on low setting.

3. Add the remaining 2 tablespoons of olive oil to the skillet. Place the skillet over very low heat, and pour in the egg and spinach mixture. Do not stir, allowing the frittata to cook slowly. As the egg mixture begins to set, distribute the olives, artichoke hearts, bacon, and basil over the top. Using a fork, gently press the toppings into the frittata. Cover the skillet with a lid and cook until the frittata is nearly firm, about 8 to 10 minutes.

4. Remove the frittata from the stove top and sprinkle with the shredded cheese. Place the frittata under the broiler, watching closely that it does not burn. Broil 3 to 5 minutes, until the eggs are cooked through and the cheese is lightly golden and bubbly.

5. Serve immediately, cut into pie-shaped wedges, with toast and fried potatoes.

VARIATION

You can substitute 2 prepared (10-ounce) boxes of frozen spinach, collard greens, or kale for the fresh spinach, and cubed salmon or cooked, crumbled sausage can be substituted for the chopped bacon.

Anna Fariello
Department of Interdisciplinary Studies
Virginia Tech, Blacksburg

Crustless Vegetable Quiche

Serves 6.

3 tablespoons butter

1 medium onion, chopped

1 cup thinly sliced zucchini

1 cup thinly sliced yellow squash

1 medium carrot, grated

1 medium tomato, cored and chopped

2 eggs, lightly beaten

1 cup cottage cheese

$\frac{1}{4}$ cup whole milk

$\frac{1}{4}$ teaspoon salt

$\frac{1}{8}$ teaspoon soy sauce

$\frac{1}{4}$ cup grated Parmesan cheese

1. Melt the butter in a non-stick skillet and sauté the onion, zucchini, and yellow squash until tender, about 5 minutes. Add the carrot and tomato and sauté an additional 3 minutes. Set the vegetables aside to cool.

2. Preheat the oven to 375°F. Lightly grease an 8x8x2-inch baking dish.

3. In a mixing bowl, stir the eggs, cottage cheese, milk, salt, and soy sauce until smooth. Spoon sautéed vegetables into the baking dish, then cover with the egg mixture.

4. Bake for 25 to 35 minutes, until firm and lightly browned. Remove from the oven and sprinkle with grated cheese. Serve immediately.

Joie Carter, Senior Fiscal Technician
VMFA, Richmond

Goat Cheese and Onion Tart

**Serves 6 as a light entrée,
or 8 as an appetizer.**

1 teaspoon butter

1 medium onion, finely diced

1 teaspoon granulated sugar

1 (10-inch) unbaked pie shell

6 eggs

1 cup heavy cream

6 ounces crumbled goat cheese

6 large leaves fresh basil, cut into chiffonade
   (finely slivered)

1. Melt the butter in a skillet. Add the chopped onion and sprinkle with the sugar. Sauté over low heat until the onion is golden brown, about 15 minutes. Set aside to cool.

2. Preheat the oven to 325°F. Bake the pie shell until lightly browned, about 10 minutes.

3. In a mixing bowl, beat the eggs lightly, then stir in the cream. Place the crumbled goat cheese in the bottom of the pie shell, sprinkle with the basil, then spoon in the sautéed onion.

4. Pour the egg mixture over the other ingredients and bake for approximately 25 minutes, until firm.

**Danny Ayers, Executive Chef
VMFA, Richmond**

CHAPTER 3
SPECIALTY SOUPS
AND SALADS

Fried Green Tomatoes and Blue Crab Salad with Buttermilk–Blue Cheese Dressing

Serves 8 as a first course, or 4 as a luncheon entrée.

In this elegant dish from Richmond's Jefferson Hotel, fried green tomatoes serve as a base for a salad of crabmeat and baby greens, topped with a creamy dressing and toasted pecans. The hotel's kitchen makes bread crumbs from "Billy Bread," a popular sourdough baked in Richmond that produces delicious bread crumbs. In this recipe, the tomatoes are marinated for added flavor, and frozen before they are fried so that they are extra crispy on the outside, and juicy on the inside. And of course, you can prepare the fried green tomatoes on their own—a classic Southern side dish.

For the Fried Green Tomatoes
The Marinade
2 cups rice wine vinegar
1/2 cup water
1/4 cup chopped fresh basil
2 tablespoons granulated sugar

6 green tomatoes, sliced 1/4-inch thick
1/2 cup kosher salt
3 tablespoons freshly ground white pepper

3 cups all-purpose flour
4 cups fine, fresh bread crumbs
5 eggs
2 cups buttermilk
2 cups canola oil for frying

1. Whisk together the vinegar, water, basil, and sugar. Layer the sliced tomatoes evenly in a shallow casserole dish and cover with the marinade. Marinate for at least 30 minutes, then drain the tomatoes thoroughly. Discard the marinade. Place the tomato slices on a large cutting board or platter and season with the kosher salt and white pepper.

2. Line a cookie sheet with waxed or parchment paper and set aside. Place the flour in a shallow bowl, then place the bread crumbs in another shallow bowl for coating the tomatoes. In a third bowl, beat the eggs with the buttermilk.

3. One at a time, lightly dust each tomato slice with flour, dip it into the egg mixture, then drop the slice into the bread crumbs, coating generously. Transfer each slice to the lined cookie sheet as you go.

4. Place the cookie sheet in the freezer and allow the tomatoes to freeze. Meanwhile, prepare the blue crab salad and buttermilk–blue cheese dressing.

For the Buttermilk–Blue Cheese Dressing

1 cup crumbled Maytag blue cheese, divided

4 cups sour cream

$\frac{1}{2}$ cup buttermilk

2 tablespoons finely minced fresh garlic

2 tablespoons apple cider vinegar

2 tablespoons Worcestershire sauce

$\frac{1}{4}$ cup finely chopped fresh basil

$\frac{1}{4}$ cup minced fresh chives

Reserve $\frac{1}{2}$ cup crumbled blue cheese. In a large mixing bowl, whisk all the remaining ingredients together until smooth, then gently fold in the reserved blue cheese. Cover and refrigerate until ready to assemble the salad. Makes 6 cups.

For the Blue Crab Salad

4 cups baby salad greens, such as mesclun mix or sunflower shoots

1 pound jumbo lump blue crabmeat, picked over for any shell bits

$\frac{1}{4}$ cup extra-virgin olive oil, or more to taste

Juice of half a lemon (about 2 tablespoons)

Salt and freshly ground white pepper to taste

1 cup lightly toasted pecan halves, for garnish

Place the salad greens and crabmeat in a large salad bowl. Drizzle with the olive oil and lemon juice and toss to combine. Season to taste with salt and pepper.

To Assemble the Salad

1. To fry the tomatoes, heat the canola oil in a heavy skillet over medium-high heat until it reaches 325°F. (You can use an "instant read" cooking thermometer to determine when the oil is hot enough—the frozen tomatoes should sizzle when they are added to the pan.) Fry the tomatoes in batches, turning once, until golden brown. Drain on paper towels and let them cool slightly.

2. Cut each fried tomato in half and arrange the halves on 8 salad plates in pinwheel designs. Mound a serving of the blue crab salad in the center of each pinwheel, then drizzle with buttermilk-blue cheese dressing. Garnish with pecan halves.

The Jefferson Hotel, Richmond
Courtesy VMFA, Richmond

Hot German Potato Salad

Serves 10 to 12.

This is an old family recipe that is a staff favorite at Explore Park in Roanoke.

The vinegar used in this recipe is "infused" with fresh dill, so place the dill sprigs in the vinegar the day before you plan to prepare the potato salad.

2 sprigs fresh dill
1½ cups distilled white vinegar
12 ounces bacon, diced
7 to 8 medium potatoes, peeled and cut into 1-inch
   cubes
1 medium onion, chopped
Salt and freshly ground pepper to taste

1. Place the dill sprigs in the vinegar, cover, and set aside overnight.

2. In a large skillet or Dutch oven, brown the diced bacon. Add the potatoes and sauté the mixture until the potatoes are nearly fork tender, about 20 to 25 minutes. Add the onion and continue to sauté the mixture 15 minutes more, or until the onion is golden brown.

3. Remove the dill sprigs from the vinegar, then pour the vinegar over the potatoes. Simmer until the potatoes are soft and the liquid has evaporated. Season to taste with salt and pepper and serve immediately.

Kimberly Burnette-Dean, Lead Interpreter
Virginia's Explore Park, Roanoke

Nineteenth-Century Chicken Salad

Serves 4.

The original recipe below is from Elizabeth E. Lea in *Domestic Cookery, Useful Receipts, and Hints to Young Housekeepers*, published by Cushings and Bailey, Baltimore, 1853:

"Cut up the white parts of a cold chicken, season it with oil or drawn butter, mustard, pepper, salt, and celery, chopped very fine, and a little vinegar. Turkey salad is made in the same manner as above."

For Drawn Butter
"Put half a pint of water in a skillet, rub a quarter of a pound of butter in a large spoonful of flour; when the water boils, stir it in and let it boil a few minutes; season it with parsley, chopped fine."

Adapted Recipe
1 tablespoon olive oil
1 teaspoon prepared mustard
$\frac{1}{4}$ teaspoon salt
$\frac{1}{4}$ teaspoon pepper
2 tablespoons vinegar (cider or white wine vinegar)
1 pound cooked boneless, skinless chicken breast (char-grilled, shredded, and chilled)
$\frac{1}{2}$ cup chopped celery

In a medium mixing bowl, whisk together the olive oil, mustard, salt, pepper, and vinegar. Add the shredded chicken and celery and toss to combine. Chill briefly before serving.

Virginia's Explore Park, Roanoke

Couscous Salad

Serves 4.

$\frac{1}{2}$ cup fresh lemon juice

Finely grated zest of one lemon

$\frac{2}{3}$ cup extra-virgin olive oil

1 teaspoon salt

$\frac{1}{2}$ teaspoon freshly ground pepper

$1\frac{1}{2}$ teaspoons minced fresh garlic

1 recipe Vegetable-Studded Couscous (see recipe index)

8 ounces cooked chicken breast, diced (optional)

1. Whisk together the lemon juice, zest, olive oil, salt, pepper, and garlic.

2. Pour the mixture over the prepared Vegetable-Studded Couscous, add the chicken, and toss to combine. Cover and refrigerate, then bring to room temperature before serving.

Linda Blake, Gallery Manager
Artisans Center of Virginia, Waynesboro

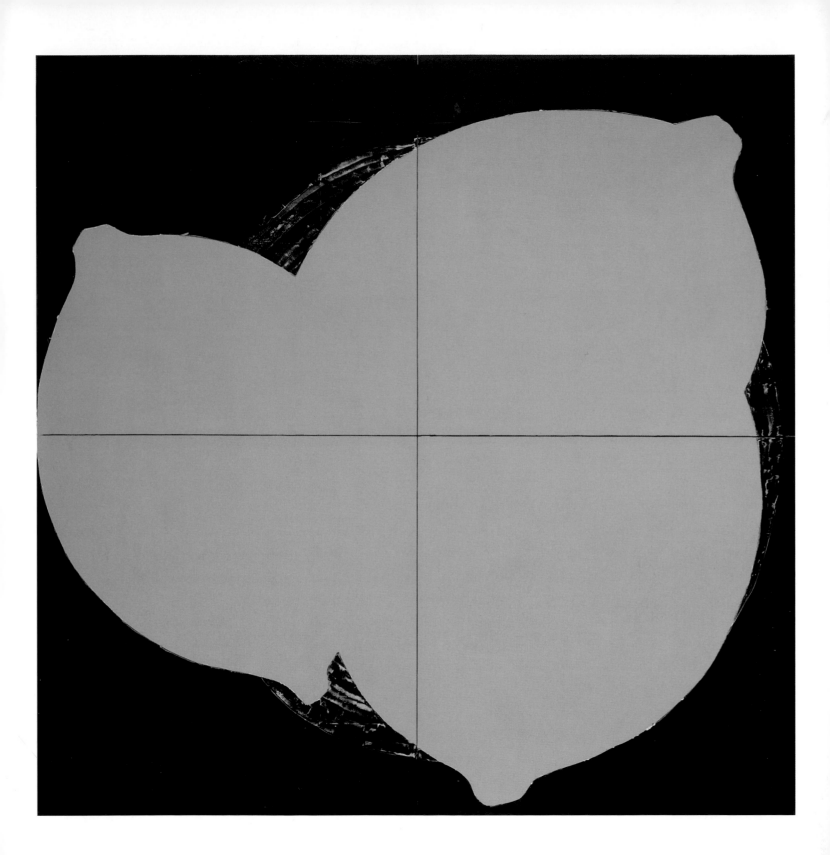

Lemon-Lime Gelatin Salad

Serves 8.

"This is a favorite family recipe that has been made for holiday meals as long as I can remember. I'm sure it must have originally been published in the 1940s or 1950s in a woman's magazine!" says Barbara Rothermel of Lynchburg.

1 (3-ounce) package lemon-flavored gelatin
1 (3-ounce) package lime-flavored gelatin
1 cup boiling water
1 pound cottage cheese
1 cup whipping cream
1 (16-ounce) can crushed pineapple, well drained
1/2 cup chopped pecans
1 tablespoon prepared horseradish
1 cup mayonnaise

1. Stir the gelatin with the boiling water until dissolved.

2. Place the cottage cheese in a blender or food processor and pulse until smooth. Stir the cottage cheese into the gelatin mixture.

3. Whip the cream and gently stir in the pineapple, pecans, horseradish, and mayonnaise. Fold in the gelatin and cottage cheese mixture.

4. Spoon the salad into a ring mold or other decorative mold, smooth with a spatula, cover with plastic wrap, and chill until firm, about 4 hours or overnight.

5. To serve, dip the mold in hot water for a few seconds, then invert it onto a bed of bright salad greens. Serve immediately.

**Barbara Rothermel, Director
Daura Gallery/Museum Studies Program
Lynchburg College**

Slaw for Fifty People

Other crunchy vegetables, such as chopped broccoli and green or red bell peppers, can be added to this basic recipe for enhanced color and flavor. Not expecting fifty? "Slaw for Six" follows (see below).

8 pounds green cabbage
1 pound carrots, peeled and finely diced
1 bunch celery, finely diced
1 pound apples (Granny Smith or Golden Delicious variety), cored and finely diced
4 cups (1 quart) mayonnaise
1 cup cider vinegar
$\frac{1}{2}$ cup granulated sugar
1 teaspoon salt

1. Grate the cabbage into an oversized mixing bowl. Add the carrots, celery, and apples.

2. In another bowl, combine the mayonnaise, vinegar, sugar, and salt. Pour the mixture over the slaw and toss to combine. Cover and chill before serving.

Slaw for Six
1 $\frac{1}{2}$ pounds grated green cabbage
2 carrots, peeled and finely diced
2 stalks celery, finely diced
1 apple, cored and finely diced
1 cup mayonnaise
3 tablespoons cider vinegar
2 tablespoons granulated sugar
Salt to taste

Prepare as directed above.

Agnes Carter, Council Member
VMFA, Richmond

This is a tasty slaw recipe that has been used for several generations.

58

Homemade Pickles

Makes 4 to 6 cups.

4 to 5 large cucumbers, unpeeled, cut into very thin
    rounds
2 cups white wine
2 cups white wine vinegar
2 tablespoons salt
2 tablespoons coarsely ground black pepper
$3/4$ cup granulated sugar
$1/4$ cup mustard seeds
1 bunch fresh dill, chopped with stems (about 1 cup)
$1/2$ bunch fresh parsley, chopped (about $1/2$ cup)
6 shallots, minced

1. Place sliced cucumbers in a large bowl and set aside.

2. Combine wine and vinegar in a saucepan and bring to boil. Add all the remaining ingredients and stir until the sugar is dissolved.

3. Pour the hot wine and vinegar mixture over the cucumber slices and fold gently to coat. Store the pickles covered in their liquid in glass jars, or other airtight containers, in the refrigerator. Serve chilled.

The pickles will retain their crispness for about one week—so enjoy them quickly.

Recipe Note

These pickles are great as a before-dinner relish, with sandwiches, or packed to accompany a picnic.

J. Frank, Personal Chef to Frances Lewis
VMFA, Richmond

"Creamless" Asparagus Soup with Spring Morels, Caramelized Shallots, and Blue Crab

Serves 6 to 8.

For the Soup

1 tablespoon olive oil

3 tablespoons chopped leeks, white part only

2 tablespoons minced shallots

1 stalk celery, diced

1 medium carrot, peeled and diced

1 teaspoon minced fresh garlic

2 pounds fresh, thin asparagus spears, cut into
      1- to-2-inch pieces, tips reserved

6 cups chicken or vegetable stock

2 bay leaves (fresh, if available)

$1\frac{1}{4}$ teaspoons mustard seeds

$\frac{3}{4}$ teaspoon kosher salt

$\frac{1}{4}$ teaspoon freshly ground white pepper

2 medium Yukon Gold potatoes, peeled and
      roughly chopped

2 tablespoons dry cooking sherry

8 ounces jumbo lump blue crabmeat, picked over
      for any shell bits

For the Garnishes

1 tablespoon olive oil

8 to 10 shallots, peeled and halved

4 ounces morel mushrooms, thoroughly rinsed and
      dried

Reserved asparagus tips (from above)

1. Heat one tablespoon olive oil in a large saucepan or soup pot. Add the leeks, minced shallots, celery, carrot, and garlic and sauté over medium heat for 3 to 4 minutes. Add the asparagus spears (reserving the tips) and cook for an additional 4 to 5 minutes, stirring occasionally.

2. Add the stock, bay leaves, mustard seeds, salt, pepper, and potatoes. Bring to a boil, reduce heat, and simmer for approximately 15 minutes, or until the asparagus and potatoes are tender.

3. Remove the bay leaves and purée the soup thoroughly in a blender or food processor. Strain the soup through a fine wire mesh colander or strainer, discarding any solids, and return the soup to the saucepan. Stir in the sherry and the crabmeat and keep the soup hot while you prepare the garnishes.

4. Prepare the garnishes by sautéeing the shallots in the heated olive oil over medium heat until they begin to brown. Add the morels and continue cooking until they are tender. Meanwhile, bring a small saucepan of water to a boil and blanch the asparagus

Cold Blueberry Soup

Makes 6 cups.

This is a wonderful summer soup, and it's incredibly easy to make.

You can make as much or as little as you like—the trick is to use equal parts of all the ingredients.

2 cups fresh orange juice
2 cups buttermilk
2 cups fresh blueberries

Simply stir all the ingredients together and chill before serving.

Dr. Steve Arbury, Director
Radford University Art Museum

Summertime Fruit Soup

Serves 4.

$\frac{1}{2}$ cup seeded and diced cantaloupe or honeydew melon
$\frac{1}{2}$ cup strawberries or raspberries
$\frac{1}{2}$ cup cranberry juice
$\frac{1}{2}$ cup orange or apple juice
$\frac{1}{2}$ cup pineapple juice
1 ripe banana
$\frac{1}{2}$ cup plain yogurt
$\frac{1}{2}$ cup heavy cream

Stir all the ingredients together, then purée in a blender or food processor. Cover and chill. Serve very cold, garnished with thin sliced fruit or sprigs of mint.

Gloria Barbre, Studio 210 Art Wearables
Torpedo Factory Art Center, Alexandria

Corn and Crab Chowder

Serves 6 to 8.

2 tablespoons butter

2 tablespoons diced onion

2 tablespoons diced celery

2 tablespoons diced red bell pepper

2 tablespoons diced green bell pepper

2 tablespoons all-purpose flour

6 cups crab or lobster broth (fish bouillon may be used)

1/2 cup diced, peeled potatoes

3/4 cup corn kernels, fresh or frozen

1 bay leaf

1/2 teaspoon Old Bay Seasoning, or more to taste

1/4 cup heavy cream

8 ounces fresh cooked crabmeat, picked over for shell bits

1 tablespoon fresh chopped chives for garnish

1. In a soup pot or large saucepan, melt the butter over medium heat. Add the onion, celery, and red and green bell peppers, and sauté until the vegetables are tender, about 10 minutes.

2. Sprinkle the flour over the vegetables, stir well, and sauté 5 minutes more. Add the broth and stir again. Add the potatoes, corn, bay leaf, and Old Bay Seasoning and bring the soup to a boil. Reduce the heat and simmer until the potatoes are tender but still firm, about 12 to 15 minutes.

3. Stir in the cream and the crabmeat and heat through. Serve immediately, garnished with chives.

The Jefferson Hotel, Richmond
Courtesy VMFA, Richmond

Creamy Brie and Mushroom Soup

Serves 4 to 6.

For the Roux

2 tablespoons unsalted butter

2 tablespoons all-purpose flour

¼ cup (½ stick) unsalted butter

2 pounds fresh mushrooms, sliced

4 cups (1 quart) half-and-half or light cream

½ large wheel of Brie (8 ounces), chilled and cut into 1-inch cubes with rind intact

6 beef bouillon cubes

½ cup dry white wine

1 tablespoon prepared roux, or more, to thicken

1. To prepare the roux, melt 2 tablespoons of butter in a small saucepan, add the flour and whisk constantly over medium heat for 5 minutes. Set the roux aside until ready to add to the soup.

2. Melt 4 tablespoons of butter in a large skillet over medium heat. Add the mushrooms and sauté until tender. Set aside.

3. In large soup pot, bring the half-and-half or cream to a near simmer over medium heat. Add the Brie and bouillon cubes and stir. As the Brie melts, the rind will separate and rise to the top. Skim the rind off the surface of the soup and discard.

4. Add the wine to the soup and briskly whisk in 1 tablespoon of roux to thicken. Add more roux, a teaspoon at a time, if desired, for a thicker consistency. Continue whisking over medium heat until the soup is hot and thickened.

5. Add the sautéed mushrooms, along with any pan juices, and serve immediately.

Danny Ayers, Executive Chef
VMFA, Richmond

CHAPTER 4
VEGETABLES
AND SIDE DISHES

Fresh Corn and Black Bean Salad

Serves 6

For the Vinaigrette

$1/3$ cup balsamic vinegar

1 tablespoon prepared sweet hot mustard

$1/4$ cup chopped fresh parsley

$1/4$ teaspoon freshly ground pepper

$1/2$ teaspoon Creole seasoning (see recipe note)

$1/4$ cup extra-virgin olive oil

$1\frac{1}{2}$ cups fresh corn kernels, cut from steamed ears of corn

8 ounces canned black beans or black-eyed peas, drained and rinsed

1 medium red onion, chopped

3 stalks celery, chopped

Whisk together the vinegar, mustard, parsley, pepper, and Creole seasoning. Whisk in the olive oil, then toss with vegetables. Cover and refrigerate before serving.

Recipe Note

If you do not have a ready-made bottle of Creole seasoning, mix equal parts garlic powder, cayenne pepper, and paprika as a substitute. This recipe can be served on a bed of Boston lettuce leaves, or as a salsa-style dip, accompanied by taco chips.

Joie Carter, Senior Fiscal Technician
VMFA, Richmond

Creamy Lemon Rice

Serves 8.

3 cups chicken stock

$1/2$ cup (1 stick) butter

2 cups long-grain rice

Zest of 2 lemons, finely grated

$1/2$ teaspoon salt

2 tablespoons fresh lemon juice

1 cup heavy cream

Freshly ground black pepper to taste

1. Bring the chicken stock to a boil; meanwhile, melt the butter in a separate heavy saucepan with a tight-fitting lid. Add the rice and lemon zest to the butter and cook over medium heat, stirring, until the rice is opaque, about 5 minutes.

2. Stir the hot chicken stock and salt into the rice. Cover and gently simmer on medium-low heat until the rice is tender, about 20 minutes.

3. Add the lemon juice and cream and continue to cook, gently stirring the rice, until the cream is absorbed, about 5 minutes. Season to taste with pepper and additional salt, if needed.

Cathy Turner
Head of Food Services and Special Events
VMFA, Richmond

Ginny's Wild Rice

Serves 4 to 6.

4 tablespoons (1/4 stick) butter
1 pound fresh mushrooms, sliced
1 cup wild rice, well-rinsed and drained
1/2 cup slivered almonds
2 tablespoons chopped fresh chives
3 cups chicken or turkey stock

1. Preheat the oven to 375°F. Melt 2 tablespoons of the butter in a skillet. Add the mushrooms and sauté until they begin to brown, about 7 to 10 minutes. Scrape the mushrooms into a 1 1/2-quart, ovenproof casserole dish with a tight-fitting lid.

2. Melt the remaining 2 tablespoons of butter in the skillet and add the rice, almonds, and chives. Sauté just until the almonds are lightly brown, then scrape the mixture into the casserole with the sautéed mushrooms.

3. In a large saucepan, bring the stock to a full boil, then carefully pour it into the casserole with the rice and mushrooms. Stir briefly to combine, then cover and bake for 1 1/2 hours, or until the rice is tender.

Virginia Gooch
Artisans Center of Virginia, Waynesboro

Saffron Rice with Pine Nuts

Serves 4.

2 tablespoons olive oil
2 tablespoons minced onion
2 tablespoons pine nuts
1 cup short or medium-grain rice (or Arborio rice)
1 cup chicken stock
1 cup water
2 tablespoons minced fresh parsley
1 1/2 teaspoons minced fresh thyme leaves
    (or 1/4 teaspoon dried)
Pinch of saffron, crumbled
Salt to taste

1. Preheat the oven to 400°F. Heat the olive oil in an ovenproof casserole dish with a tight-fitting lid. Sauté the onion and pine nuts until just golden, about 5 minutes.

2. Add the rice and stir until it is coated with olive oil. Stir in the chicken stock, water, parsley, thyme, saffron, and salt. Bring to a boil, cover, and transfer the casserole to the oven. Bake 15 minutes, then remove the casserole from the oven and allow the rice to sit for 5 to 10 minutes before serving.

Suzanne Freeman
Head Librarian and Publications Manager
VMFA, Richmond

Vegetable-Studded Couscous

Serves 4.

3 tablespoons butter

1 medium yellow onion, finely diced

2 teaspoons minced fresh garlic, or more to taste

1 red bell pepper, seeded and finely diced

2 carrots, peeled and finely diced

2 teaspoons minced fresh rosemary leaves

1 cup quick-cooking couscous

1¾ cups chicken stock

¼ teaspoon salt

½ teaspoon fresh ground pepper

½ teaspoon turmeric

½ of a Granny Smith Apple, cored and finely diced

¼ cup chopped scallions (green onions)

2 tablespoons minced fresh parsley

⅓ cup raisins

½ cup canned garbanzo beans, drained

1. Melt the butter in a large saucepan or skillet. Add the onion and sauté for 3 minutes.

2. Add the garlic, bell pepper, carrots, and rosemary. Sauté 5 minutes longer. Add the couscous and toss with the vegetables. Add the chicken stock, salt, pepper, and turmeric.

3. Continue cooking, stirring constantly, for 2 minutes or until the liquid is absorbed. Remove the pan from the heat and stir in the apple, scallions (green onions), parsley, raisins, and garbanzo beans. Serve immediately.

Linda Blake, Gallery Manager
Artisans Center of Virginia, Waynesboro

Asparagus Timbales

Serves 8.

These asparagus custards, or "timbales," are baked in a water bath.

To prepare the water bath, bring a large, full kettle of water to a boil. Place a roasting pan large enough to hold eight 6-ounce custard cups in the preheated oven, arrange the filled cups in the roasting pan, then pour in enough boiling water to reach halfway up the sides of the custard cups. Bake as directed, removing the roasting pan carefully when the timbales are done.

2 pounds fresh asparagus spears, trimmed and cut
    into 2-inch pieces
6 egg yolks
$1/3$ cup heavy cream
$1/3$ cup finely grated Parmesan cheese
2 cloves garlic, roughly chopped
Salt and pepper to taste

Vegetable oil for custard cups

1. Bring a large pot of lightly salted water to a full boil. Cook the asparagus until it is very soft, about 10 to 12 minutes. Drain the asparagus and set aside to cool.

2. Place the cooked asparagus and all the remaining ingredients in the bowl of a food processor and pulse the mixture until it is completely smooth. Lightly coat the insides of the custard cups with vegetable oil, then fill each with the timbale mixture to within $1/2$-inch of the brim of the cup.

3. Tap the cups gently on the work surface to remove any air bubbles, then arrange them in the roasting pan as directed above. Bake at 350°F for 30 to 45 minutes, or until fully set and firm. Carefully remove the pan from the oven and remove the timbales from the water bath.

4. To serve, run a damp knife lightly around the rim of each cup and invert onto a serving plate.

Steven Gabay, Banquet Chef
VMFA, Richmond

Bourbon Sweet Potato Casserole

Serves 6.

This is a variation of an old favorite from Barbara Parker's grandmother's recipe file.

The casserole is made the day before it is baked to allow the flavors to meld with the bourbon.

6 medium sweet potatoes or yams, cooked, skinned and mashed or 1 (28-ounce) can of yams, drained and mashed
1/2 cup melted butter
1/2 cup firmly packed brown sugar
1/3 cup orange juice
1/4 cup bourbon (or substitute Drambuie)
1/2 teaspoon salt
1/2 teaspoon pumpkin pie spice
1/2 cup chopped pecans (optional)

1. In a large mixing bowl, fold all the ingredients together until well-blended.

2. Spread the mixture in a casserole dish, cover, and chill overnight.

3. Preheat the oven to 350°F and bake the casserole for 30 minutes, or until heated through and golden brown.

**Barbara Parker, Director of Programs
Piedmont Arts Association, Martinsville**

Brewer's Sweet Potato Dish

Serves 6.

2 to 3 pounds baked sweet potatoes, peeled
3/4 cup brown sugar
1/2 cup (1 stick) butter, soft, at room temperature (plus 1 additional tablespoon soft butter for coating casserole dish)
1 teaspoon cinnamon
1/2 teaspoon nutmeg
1 cup miniature marshmallows
1/2 cup chopped walnuts
1 cup shredded sweetened coconut, divided

1. In a large mixing bowl, mash together the sweet potatoes, brown sugar, and butter. Add the cinnamon, nutmeg, marshmallow, walnuts, and 3/4 cup of the coconut. Fold the ingredients together to blend.

2. Preheat the oven to 350°F. Grease a casserole dish with the remaining tablespoon of butter. Spread the sweet potato mixture into the casserole and top with the remaining 1/4 cup coconut. Bake until heated through and golden brown, about 30 minutes.

**Leigh Anne Chambers, Executive Director
Rawls Museum Arts, Courtland**

Tar Beach (Woman on a Bridge Series Part 1) by Faith Ringgold, © 1988

Corn Pudding and Fresh "Stewed" Corn

Serves 6 to 8.

These heirloom recipes are adapted from *A Book of Recipes for the Cooking School* by Carrie Alberta Lyford, published by the Press of The Hampton Normal and Agricultural Institute in 1921. Ms. Lyford was then the Director of the Institute's Home Economics School.

2 tablespoons softened butter, divided
1 dozen ears fresh corn or 3 (16-ounce) cans of
    corn, drained
1 teaspoon granulated sugar
1/2 teaspoon salt
2 tablespoons flour
2 cups whole milk
3 eggs, separated

1. Use 1 tablespoon soft butter to grease a casserole dish and preheat the oven to 350°F.

2. If using fresh corn, scrape the kernels off the cobs into a large mixing bowl. Add the remaining tablespoon of soft butter, sugar, salt, and flour to the corn, and toss to coat.

3. In a separate bowl beat the egg yolks with the milk, then add to the corn mixture. In another bowl, beat the egg whites to form stiff peaks. Fold the eggs whites into the corn mixture. Spread the pudding into the prepared casserole dish and bake 30 to 40 minutes, or until firm.

Fresh "Stewed" Corn

"Cut the fresh corn from the cob, scraping as much pulp from the corn as possible. Season with salt and pepper, add a little milk and butter, and simmer a few minutes on top of the stove or in the oven."

Hampton University Museum

Hot Spinach Casserole

Serves 8.

2 (10-ounce) packages frozen, chopped spinach

4 tablespoons (1/2 stick) butter, divided

3 tablespoons chopped onion

2 tablespoons all-purpose flour

1/2 cup evaporated milk

1/4 teaspoon freshly ground black pepper

Dash cayenne pepper

3/4 teaspoon celery salt

3/4 teaspoon chopped fresh garlic

1 teaspoon Worcestershire sauce

6 ounces grated pepper jack cheese, or Cheddar
    cheese with jalapeño peppers

1 cup fresh bread crumbs, torn into bite-size pieces

1. Prepare the spinach according to package directions, drain well, reserving 1/2 cup cooking liquid.

2. Melt 2 tablespoons of the butter in a skillet and sauté the onion over medium heat until soft, about 5 minutes. Sprinkle on the flour and mix well.

3. Add the evaporated milk and the spinach liquid to the skillet. Add the black pepper, cayenne pepper, celery salt, garlic, and Worcestershire sauce and bring to a simmer. Add the grated cheese and stir until melted. Fold in the drained spinach.

4. Preheat the oven to 350°F. Lightly grease a casserole dish. Spread the spinach mixture into the dish.

5. In another skillet, melt the remaining 2 tablespoons of butter and sauté the bread crumbs until they are light, golden brown. Sprinkle the bread crumbs over the casserole and bake for 30 minutes, or until bubbly and lightly browned.

Lynda Johnson Robb
Former First Lady of Virginia
Courtesy McLean Project for the Arts

Roasted New Potatoes with Herbs and Balsamic Vinegar

Serves 4 to 6.

1 pound fresh new potatoes, cut into 1/2-inch cubes
5 tablespoons olive oil, divided
3 slices bacon, cut into thin strips (optional)
4 cloves fresh garlic, minced
1 tablespoon chopped fresh sage leaves
Salt and freshly ground black pepper to taste
1 tablespoon balsamic vinegar

1. Preheat the oven to 450°F. Toss the cubed potatoes with 3 tablespoons olive oil, the bacon, garlic, sage, salt, and pepper. Spread the potatoes in a single layer in a 9x9x2-inch glass baking pan. Bake for 35 to 40 minutes, stirring often, until tender and browned.

2. In a serving bowl, whisk together the remaining 2 tablespoons of olive oil with the balsamic vinegar. Scrape in the hot potatoes and toss. Season with additional salt and pepper to taste and serve immediately.

Jan Hurt
William King Regional Arts Center, Abingdon

Yellow Squash Casserole

Serves 6.

2 pounds yellow squash, cut into 1-inch cubes
1 tablespoon soft butter
1 can cream of chicken soup
1 large onion, grated
1 carrot, peeled and grated
1 cup sour cream
1 cup fine, fresh bread crumbs, divided
1/2 teaspoon salt
1/4 teaspoon freshly ground black pepper

1. Bring a large pot of lightly salted water to a boil. Add the squash and cook until very tender, about 15 minutes. Drain well.

2. Use the butter to lightly grease a casserole dish. Preheat the oven to 350°F. Place the squash in a large mixing bowl and coarsely mash with a potato masher. Add the soup, onion, carrot, sour cream, and 3/4 cup bread crumbs. Add salt and pepper and stir to combine.

3. Spread the squash mixture into the prepared casserole and top evenly with the remaining 1/4 cup bread crumbs. Bake 30 to 40 minutes, or until brown and bubbly.

Pat Featherstun, First Vice President
Piedmont Arts Association, Martinsville

Potato Stuffing for Roasted Duck or Goose

Serves 6 to 8.

This is another heirloom recipe adapted from *A Book of Recipes for the Cooking School* written by Carrie Alberta Lyford. The book was published by the Press of The Hampton Normal and Agricultural Institute in 1921, when Ms. Lyford was then the Director of the Institute's Home Economics School.

Serve alongside roasted duck or other fowl.

4 cups hot mashed potatoes (about 10 medium potatoes, peeled and boiled until soft)
2 teaspoons pressed onion juice
2 teaspoons salt
$^1/_4$ teaspoon freshly ground black pepper
2 tablespoons soft butter
2 egg yolks
$^1/_4$ cup cream
1 tablespoon minced fresh parsley

1. Mix the mashed potatoes with the onion juice, salt, pepper, and butter.

2. In a small bowl, beat the egg yolks with the cream, then add the mixture to the potatoes. Add the parsley and stir to combine.

3. Use this mixture to stuff a duck or goose before roasting, or place in a buttered dish, and bake it at 350°F for 45 minutes or until brown on top.

Hampton University Museum

CHAPTER 5
SEAFOOD

Greek Shrimp and Rice

Serves 8.

This recipe was originally published in the VMFA Council's first cookbook in 1992.

For the Greek-style Rice

$\frac{1}{4}$ cup olive oil

$\frac{1}{2}$ cup chopped onion

1 cup pine nuts

2 cups long-grain rice

2 (14 $\frac{1}{2}$-ounce) cans chicken broth

1 cup crumbled feta cheese

6 tablespoons minced fresh mint leaves (or
    2 tablespoons dried mint)

Salt and freshly ground pepper to taste

For the Shrimp

6 tablespoons olive oil

$\frac{2}{3}$ cup chopped onion

2 (28-ounce) cans Italian plum tomatoes, drained
    and chopped

1 cup dry white wine

2 teaspoons dried oregano

2 cups sliced fresh mushrooms

2 pounds fresh, raw shrimp, peeled and deveined

Salt and freshly ground pepper to taste

1. To prepare the rice, heat the olive oil in a medium-sized, heavy saucepan. Add the onion and pine nuts and sauté over medium heat until the onion is translucent, about 8 minutes. Add the rice and broth and bring to a boil. Reduce heat to low, cover, and cook until the broth is absorbed, about 20 minutes. Before serving, fluff with a fork and add the cheese and mint. Season with salt and pepper to taste.

2. To prepare the shrimp, heat the olive oil in a large, heavy skillet and sauté the onion over medium heat until translucent, about 8 minutes. Add the tomatoes, wine, and oregano, and simmer until thickened, about 5 to 10 minutes. Add the mushrooms and shrimp and cook about 4 minutes longer, until the shrimp are opaque and heated through. Season with salt and pepper to taste. Serve immediately, spooned over the hot rice.

The Council
VMFA, Richmond

Chesapeake Bay Oyster Stew with Mascarpone Grits, Forest Mushrooms, and Black Pepper Demi-Glace

Serves 5 to 7.

The grits in this dish are from Byrd Mill in Ashland. They are ground at a very low temperature over a coarse granite stone that preserves the corn flavor. These are not your everyday "instant" grits. They need to simmer for approximately 4 hours and therefore need frequent stirring and attention until they are tender and evenly cooked.

In this recipe from the Jefferson Hotel in Richmond, the grits are cooked in milk and finished with mascarpone cheese (a sweet Italian cream cheese).

The "stew" portion of this recipe, which is spooned over the finished grits to complete the dish, should not be made until you are ready to serve to your guests.

The forest mushrooms used in the hotel's kitchen vary according to seasonal availability. Most likely, the varieties will consist of shiitake, oyster, black trumpet, and golden chanterelle mushrooms.

For the Grits

½ cup Byrd Mill Stoneground Grits

1½ cups whole milk, and up to 1 cup additional

1 fresh bay leaf

3 tablespoons Plugrá brand butter (or any unsalted butter)

Salt and fresh-ground white pepper to taste

2 tablespoons mascarpone cheese

For the Stew

1 tablespoon Plugrá brand butter (or any unsalted butter)

1 medium shallot, diced

½ clove garlic, minced

½ red bell pepper, diced

½ yellow bell pepper, diced

½ green bell pepper, diced

1 cup sliced seasonal mushrooms

4 slices cooked and diced apple-wood smoked bacon

1 pint shucked Chesapeake Bay oysters, their liquor drained and reserved

1 cup prepared demi-glace (rich, reduced veal stock, available in specialty markets)

¼ cup heavy cream

2 tablespoons minced fresh herbs (any mix of parsley, chervil, tarragon, chives)

Salt and freshly ground black pepper to taste

1. For the grits, combine the first 5 ingredients in a heavy 2-quart saucepan and bring to a simmer over

low heat. Cook uncovered, stirring frequently for about 4 hours, adding milk as needed to keep a creamy consistency. When the grits are soft, remove the pan from the heat and set aside until you are ready to prepare the stew. (Just before you are ready to serve the finished dish, reheat the grits, add the mascarpone cheese, and salt and pepper to taste.)

2. To prepare the stew, melt the butter in a large skillet over medium heat. Add the shallot, garlic, bell peppers, mushrooms, and diced bacon. Sauté until the vegetables are tender, about 5 to 7 minutes.

3. Add the reserved oyster liquor and the demi-glace to the skillet and bring to a simmer, stirring, until slightly reduced, about 5 minutes, then stir in the cream and minced herbs. Season with salt and pepper to taste.

4. Reheat and finish the grits as directed above (Step 1). Add the oysters to the simmering stew until just poached and the edges begin to become ruffled, about 30 seconds. Serve the stew immediately, spooned over the hot grits.

The Jefferson Hotel, Richmond
Courtesy VMFA, Richmond

Oyster and Eggplant Casserole

Serves 4 to 6.

This recipe is from Barbara Parker's grandmother's recipe file.

1 large eggplant, diced
2 tablespoons butter
1 medium onion, chopped
1 pint fresh, raw oysters, drained
2 cups prepared, unseasoned croutons
2 cups half-and-half

1. Bring a large pot of lightly salted water to a boil. Add the eggplant and cook until tender, about 8 to 10 minutes. Drain thoroughly in a colander and set aside.

2. Melt the butter in a skillet over medium heat. Add the onion and sauté until soft, about 8 minutes. Add the oysters and continue to sauté until they are cooked and the edges have ruffled, about 3 to 4 minutes.

3. Preheat the oven to 350°F. Lightly butter a casserole dish. Place a layer of cooked eggplant in the bottom of the casserole, then cover with half the oyster and onion mixture. Top with a layer (1 cup) of croutons. Repeat, finishing the casserole with a layer of croutons. Pour the half-and-half evenly over the casserole. Bake for 30 minutes, or until bubbly and lightly browned.

Barbara Parker, Director of Programs
Piedmont Arts Association, Martinsville

Curry Seafood Crepes

**Serves 12 as an appetizer
(1 crepe per plate), or
6 as an entrée (2 crepes per plate).**

For the Crepe Batter
4 eggs
1 cup cold milk
1 cup cold water
½ teaspoon salt
2 teaspoons granulated sugar
2 cups sifted all-purpose flour
¼ cup (½ stick) melted unsalted butter, plus
    additional for frying
2 tablespoons cognac (optional)

1. Put the eggs in a blender or the bowl of a food processor and pulse briefly. Add the milk, water, salt, and sugar and pulse a few times to blend. With the motor running, slowly add a spoonful of flour at a time, then add the melted butter. Blend or pulse until the batter is smooth and is the consistency of heavy cream. Cover and refrigerate for 1 hour before making the crepes.

2. To fry 12 crepes, use a crepe pan or flat, heavy-bottomed skillet. For each crepe heat the skillet and brush with melted butter. Pour ¼ cup of batter into the center. Swirl the batter to make a thin, 6-inch-wide crepe. When the surface of the crepe begins to bubble and the edges begin to curl, flip the crepe and very lightly brown the other side. Total cooking time should be just 1 to 2 minutes.

3. Stack the cooked crepes on a platter, cover them with foil and keep them warm in a 225°F oven until you are ready to assemble the finished dish. (Crepes can also be refrigerated or frozen in a zip-lock bag for later use.)

For the Curry Seafood Filling
1 tablespoon extra-virgin olive oil
1 cup diced onion
1 cup diced red bell pepper
2 stalks celery, diced
1 cup sliced mushrooms
2 cups heavy cream
2 tablespoons curry powder
1 teaspoon mixed dried herbs such as dill, tarragon,
    chives, and parsley (or use any special herb
    blend for seasoning fish and seafood)
Salt and fresh-ground pepper to taste
8 ounces fresh raw shrimp, peeled and deveined
8 ounces fresh crabmeat, picked over for any shell
    bits (reserve liquid)
½ cup finely grated Parmigiano-Reggiano cheese

1. Heat the olive oil in a large skillet over medium heat. Add the onion, bell pepper, and celery and sauté until crisp-tender, about 7 to 10 minutes. Add the mushrooms and sauté until soft, about 5 minutes more.

2. Whisk in the cream, curry powder, and herbs. Bring the mixture to a simmer and cook, uncovered, for 8 to 10 minutes to reduce and thicken the sauce. Season with salt and pepper to taste. Add the shrimp and crabmeat and cook just until the shrimp are opaque and the mixture is heated through, 3 to 5 minutes.

3. To assemble the crepes, place each on a warmed dinner plate, "good" side down. Place 2 to 3 tablespoons of filling into the center of the crepe. Roll the crepe so that it lies seam-side down on the plate, then place an additional tablespoon of the filling and sauce over the top. Dust lightly with grated cheese and serve immediately.

Recipe Note

To prepare ahead of time, place the filled crepes in a shallow, buttered baking dish, cover with plastic wrap, and refrigerate. To serve, preheat the oven to 350°F and bake the crepes for 20 to 30 minutes, until heated through. Dust the crepes with grated cheese and place under the broiler briefly to lightly brown the tops.

**Bill White, Painter and Professor of Art
Hollins University, Roanoke**

Bacon-Wrapped Scallops in Cherry Brandy Cream Sauce

Serves 4.

2 cups heavy cream

1/2 cup cherry brandy

1 to 1 1/2 pounds fresh sea scallops (about 12 large scallops)

Salt and coarsely ground black pepper to taste

12 thick slices peppered bacon (about 1 pound)

2 tablespoons extra-virgin olive oil

1/4 teaspoon mild paprika

1/4 cup chopped fresh basil, plus 12 whole leaves of fresh basil for garnish

1. In a heavy saucepan, bring the cream to a gentle simmer over low heat. Whisk in the brandy and continue to simmer, whisking, until the sauce is reduced and thickened, about 10 to 15 minutes. Set aside and keep warm until you are ready to serve the scallops.

2. Rinse the scallops and pat them dry, then season them with a few pinches of salt and pepper. Roll each scallop in a slice of bacon and secure it with a short bamboo skewer or sturdy toothpick.

3. Heat the olive oil in a medium skillet. Add the scallops, sprinkle with the paprika, and sauté over low heat, turning frequently, until the scallops are opaque and the bacon is browned and the edges are crisp. Add the chopped basil and toss to combine. Remove the scallops from the skillet and drain on a rack or paper towels.

4. To serve, place 3 scallops on each serving plate in a pool of the warm Cherry Brandy Cream Sauce, and garnish with fresh basil leaves on the edge of the plate.

Dr. Richard Bay
Radford University Art Museum

Macadamia Nut and Sesame-Crusted Grouper with Soy Butter Sauce

Serves 8.

This recipe uses Japanese Panko bread crumbs favored increasingly by chefs internationally because of the satisfying extra-crunchy texture they add to fried or baked foods. Panko bread crumbs are sold in specialty grocery and seafood markets, or via the internet.

For the Soy Butter Sauce

¼ cup light soy sauce

½ teaspoon sesame oil

⅛ teaspoon ground ginger

¼ cup dry white wine

1 shallot, minced

1 clove fresh garlic, minced

1 cup (2 sticks) butter, chilled and cut into
   tablespoon-sized cubes

For the Grouper

1 cup Panko bread crumbs

¼ cup finely chopped unsalted macadamia nuts

⅛ teaspoon golden sesame seeds

⅛ teaspoon black sesame seeds (optional)

⅛ teaspoon ground ginger

⅛ teaspoon granulated garlic

¼ cup melted butter

8 (5-ounce) grouper fillets, picked over for any pin
   bones

3 tablespoons olive or canola oil

½ teaspoon salt

¼ teaspoon fresh-ground pepper

1. Place the soy sauce, sesame oil, ginger, wine, shallot, and garlic in a small saucepan. Bring to a simmer, stirring, and cook 3 to 5 minutes. Remove the pan from the heat and whisk in the butter, a tablespoon at a time, until melted.

2. In a mixing bowl, combine the bread crumbs, macadamia nuts, sesame seeds, ginger, and garlic. Drizzle in the melted butter and toss to combine. Set the mixture aside.

3. Preheat the oven to 325°F. Have ready a lightly greased baking sheet. Heat the olive or canola oil in a large skillet over high heat. Season the grouper fillets with the salt and pepper. Sear them quickly in the hot oil, about 1 minute per side, then transfer them to the baking sheet.

4. Press 2 to 3 tablespoons of the bread crumb and nut mixture over each fillet to cover evenly. Bake the fillets until golden brown, about 8 to 12 minutes. Serve immediately, drizzled with warm Soy Butter Sauce.

The Jefferson Hotel, Richmond
Courtesy VMFA, Richmond

Pistachio-Crusted Rockfish

Serves 4.

10 ounces unsalted pistachios
2 tablespoons all-purpose flour
2 teaspoons garlic powder
1 teaspoon salt
1 teaspoon freshly ground pepper
4 eggs
4 (6-ounce) rockfish fillets, or other firm-fleshed fish
1/2 cup (1 stick) unsalted butter

1. Place the pistachios in a blender or the bowl of a food processor and pulse until finely chopped, but not powdered. Add the flour, garlic powder, salt, and pepper and pulse briefly to blend. Pour the pistachio mixture into a wide, shallow bowl or pie pan.

2. In a separate shallow bowl, whisk the eggs thoroughly. To coat the fish, dip each fillet into the beaten eggs, then dip into the pistachio mixture to coat completely. Press the pistachio crust firmly into the flesh of the fish and set aside on a platter or sheet of wax paper.

3. Preheat the oven to 350°F. Melt the butter in a large, heavy skillet over medium heat and add the fish fillets. Brown them lightly, turning once, approximately 3 to 4 minutes per side, then transfer to a baking sheet and bake approximately 15 minutes, until flaky and cooked through. Serve immediately.

Danny Ayers, Executive Chef
VMFA, Richmond

Norfolk-Style Salmon

Serves 6

This dish is adapted from a recipe in *A Seafood Heritage from the Rappahannock to the Rio Grande*, published by the U.S. Department of Commerce.

1/4 cup freshly squeezed lime juice
1 teaspoon dried marjoram leaves, crushed
6 salmon steaks (3/4-inch thick, about 6 ounces each)
2 tablespoons melted butter
1 teaspoon salt
1/8 teaspoon freshly ground pepper

1. Combine the lime juice and marjoram in a shallow glass dish large enough to hold all the salmon steaks in a single layer. Add the salmon steaks, turning to moisten both sides, then cover and marinate, refrigerated, at least 1 hour, turning once.

2. Prepare a hot charcoal grill, fitted with a lid or cover. Brush the salmon steaks with the melted butter, season with salt and pepper, and place them on the hot grill about 4 inches from the coals. Cover and cook approximately 10 to 15 minutes, or until the fish is browned and flakes easily when tested with a fork. (The salmon steaks need not be turned as they cook.)

Janet D. Howell , Virginia Senator
Courtesy McLean Project for the Arts

Raspberry Broiled Salmon

Serves 4.

For the Vinaigrette Marinade
2 tablespoons raspberry vinegar
1 tablespoon minced shallots
$\frac{1}{3}$ cup extra-virgin olive oil
$\frac{1}{4}$ teaspoon salt
Pinch freshly ground pepper

4 (5-ounce) fresh salmon fillets

1. To prepare the vinaigrette marinade, whisk the vinegar, shallots, olive oil, salt, and pepper together. Place the salmon in a glass dish that will hold all the fillets in a single layer. Pour the vinaigrette over the salmon, coating well. Cover and marinate in the refrigerator for at least 30 minutes.

2. Preheat the broiler. Remove the salmon from the vinaigrette. Place the fillets on a foil-lined baking sheet and broil 2 to 4 inches from heat for 10 to 12 minutes, or until the salmon flakes easily with a fork.

Mira Totskaya
VMFA, Richmond

Grilled-Tuna Salad Niçoise

Serves 2.

For the Dressing
3 tablespoons fresh-squeezed lemon juice
1 clove garlic, minced
1 teaspoon fresh chopped oregano leaves
$\frac{1}{2}$ cup good quality olive oil
Salt and freshly ground pepper to taste

6 ounces haricots verts
6 ounces mixed salad greens or mesclun mix
2 char-grilled tuna steaks (1-inch thick, about
    6 ounces each)
6 small new potatoes, cooked until tender, then
    chilled
$\frac{1}{2}$ medium red onion, thinly sliced
2 hard-boiled eggs, peeled and quartered
2 medium-ripe tomatoes, quartered
12 black olives, preferably Kalamata

1. Whisk the lemon juice with the garlic and oregano. Slowly drizzle in the olive oil, whisking constantly. Season the dressing with salt and pepper to taste.

2. Bring a large pot of lightly salted water to a boil. Have a large bowl of ice water ready. Drop the haricots verts in the boiling water for approximately 1 minute, just until the color brightens. Drain them in a colander and immediately plunge them into the

ice water. When the beans are cold, drain again and thoroughly dry them. Cover and refrigerate until you are ready to plate the salad.

2. Place the salad greens in a large bowl and toss lightly with half the dressing. Divide the greens between 2 dinner plates. Break each tuna steak into large pieces and place on the greens. Arrange the potatoes, onion, eggs, tomatoes, and haricots verts over the greens. Finish by garnishing the salads with the olives and drizzling on the remaining dressing to taste.

Steven Gabay, Banquet Chef
VMFA, Richmond

Raita

Serves 4 to 6.

Chilled Raita, a cooling relish, and Banana Salsa, right, are good summertime accompaniments for pan-seared, broiled, or grilled fish fillets, such as Mira Totskaya's Raspberry Broiled Salmon (see recipe index).

1 cucumber, peeled, seeded, and grated

16 ounces (2 cups) plain yogurt

1 teaspoon salt

$\frac{1}{8}$ teaspoon freshly ground pepper

$\frac{1}{2}$ teaspoon ground cumin (or whole cumin seeds, toasted)

$\frac{1}{8}$ teaspoon cayenne pepper

$\frac{1}{8}$ teaspoon paprika

Combine all the ingredients, cover, and chill before serving. To serve, spoon over hot fish fillets.

Jacqueline S. Brownfield
University of Virginia Art Museum
Charlottesville

Banana Salsa

Serves 4.

2 limes

3 tablespoons chopped fresh cilantro

2 tablespoons minced scallions (green onions)

2 tablespoons finely chopped red bell pepper

1 tablespoon honey

$\frac{1}{4}$ teaspoon hot pepper sauce, or more to taste

4 firm, ripe, medium bananas, peeled and diced

1. Using a zester or vegetable peeler, cut the zest (dark green outer peel) from the limes, then finely chop it. Squeeze the juice from the limes.

2. In a medium mixing bowl, combine the zest and lime juice with the cilantro, scallions (green onions), bell pepper, honey, and hot pepper sauce. Chill the mixture.

3. Just before serving, gently toss in the diced bananas. Serve alongside hot grilled salmon fillets.

Jacqueline S. Brownfield
University of Virginia Art Museum
Charlottesville

Governor's Crab Cakes

Serves 4 to 6.

4 tablespoons butter, divided

$\frac{1}{4}$ teaspoon minced fresh garlic

1 tablespoon minced shallots

$\frac{1}{4}$ cup minced bell pepper (red, green, or yellow, or a combination)

1 teaspoon Old Bay Seasoning (or other seafood seasoning)

1 teaspoon prepared Dijon mustard

3 drops Tabasco (or other hot pepper sauce), or more to taste

1 egg

$\frac{1}{2}$ cup mayonnaise

Fresh-squeezed juice of half a lemon (about 2 tablespoons)

1 pound jumbo lump crabmeat, picked over for any shell bits

2 tablespoons herb-seasoned fine, dry bread crumbs

$\frac{1}{4}$ cup crushed Ritz Crackers (or other buttery-style cracker)

$\frac{1}{2}$ teaspoon salt

$\frac{1}{4}$ teaspoon freshly ground white pepper, or more to taste

1. Preheat oven to 350°F. Melt 1 tablespoon of the butter in a small skillet and sauté the garlic, shallots, bell peppers, and Old Bay Seasoning over medium heat until crisp-tender, about 2 minutes.

2. In a mixing bowl, combine the Dijon mustard, Tabasco, egg, mayonnaise, and lemon juice with the cooked pepper mixture. Fold in the crabmeat, bread crumbs, and crackers. Add the salt and pepper and gently mix to combine.

4. Melt the remaining butter in a large skillet. Form the crab mixture into 1-ounce cakes (about 1 heaping tablespoon per cake) and sauté, turning once, until golden brown on each side. Transfer the crab cakes to a baking sheet and bake for 5 to 8 minutes, until firm and golden brown.

Mark W. Herndon, Executive Chef
The Governor's Executive Mansion, Richmond
Courtesy VMFA, Richmond

Maestro Lobster Ravioli with Bisque Sauce—"I Ravioli D'Astice"

Serves 4.

This elegant and elaborate dish begins with four live lobsters and results in a plate of creamy delicate ravioli garnished with chunks of lobster meat—a challenge for the ambitious at-home chef.

For the Ravioli

1/2 cup chopped onion

1/4 cup chopped fresh tarragon

1 teaspoon salt, plus additional to taste

1/2 teaspoon freshly ground pepper, plus additional to taste

4 (1 1/2-pound) live Maine lobsters

12 3x3-inch square wonton wrappers

4 tablespoons extra-virgin olive oil

2 tablespoons chopped fresh chives

1 egg, beaten

For the Bisque Sauce

Reserved carcasses of 4 lobsters

1/4 cup (1/2 stick) butter

1/4 cup chopped shallots

1/4 cup chopped carrots

1/4 cup chopped celery

3 plum tomatoes, seeded and chopped

1 1/2 teaspoons curry powder

1 tablespoon tomato paste

12 ounces (1 1/2 cups) Armagnac brandy

16 ounces (2 cups) port

1 quart (4 cups) fish stock

1 quart (4 cups) heavy cream

1/4 cup chopped fresh Italian parsley

1. Fill a lobster steaming pot, or other large stock pot, with water and bring it to a full boil. Add the onion, tarragon, 1 teaspoon salt, and 1/2 teaspoon pepper. (Have a second large pot of ice water ready to chill the lobsters after blanching.)

2. Place the lobsters in the pot two at time, blanching the first two for just 20 seconds, and the remaining two for about 1 1/2 minutes. Pull the lobsters from the boiling pot with tongs, then plunge them into the ice water. Reserve 6 cups of the blanching water and set aside.

3. Remove the claw and tail meat from the first two lobsters and reserve the carcasses. Coarsely chop the lobster meat and place it in a mixing bowl. Add 3 tablespoons of the olive oil, chopped chives, and additional salt and pepper to taste. Toss to combine.

4. Place the wonton wrappers on a flat work surface or cutting board and place about 1 tablespoon of the seasoned lobster meat in the center of each. Brush the edges of the wonton wrapper with beaten egg

and fold them into triangles, completely pressing the edges together to form a well-sealed ravioli. Transfer the ravioli to a platter, cover with plastic wrap, and refrigerate at least 20 minutes before cooking.

5. Remove the claw and tail meat from the remaining two lobsters, coarsely chop it, then toss with the remaining tablespoon of olive oil and set aside. Crush all 4 lobster carcasses into small chunks by chopping them with a heavy knife or cleaver, or by pulsing them in the bowl of a food processor fitted with a steel blade.

6. Melt the butter in a large saucepan or soup pot. Add the chopped lobster carcasses and sauté them until they begin to brown, about 10 minutes. Add the shallots, carrots, celery, and plum tomatoes and continue to sauté the mixture until the vegetables are soft and golden in color, about 10 to 15 minutes more.

7. Sprinkle the curry powder over the mixture and fold in the tomato paste. Pour in the Armagnac and stir the pot, scraping any brown bits from the bottom. Simmer and stir until the liquid is reduced by one-third. Add the port, then simmer and stir until the liquids have reduced by half.

8. Add the fish stock and allow the mixture to simmer, uncovered, for 25 to 30 minutes. Meanwhile, in another large saucepan, bring the cream to a simmer and allow it to reduce by half.

9. To finish the bisque, strain the reduced stock mixture into bowl, firmly pressing the solids to extract all the liquid. Discard the solids. Whisk the strained stock into the reduced cream, bring to a simmer, and reduce again to a thick, creamy consistency. Season to taste with salt and pepper. Keep the bisque warm while you prepare the ravioli.

10. Preheat the oven to 200°F. To reheat the reserved lobster meat, place it on a baking sheet, then cover with a towel dampened in the reserved lobster-blanching water. Warm it in the oven for about 8 to 10 minutes.

11. Meanwhile, bring the reserved blanching water to a full boil in a large stock pot. Drop in the ravioli and simmer until they rise to the top and are tender, about 5 minutes. Lift the ravioli from the boiling water with a slotted spoon and divide them among individual serving plates.

12. To finish the dish, garnish the ravioli with the warmed lobster meat. Quickly whisk the bisque sauce, then pour it generously over the ravioli. Serve immediately.

Fabio Trabocchi, Maestro Chef de Cuisine
The Ritz-Carlton, Tysons Corner
Courtesy McLean Project for the Arts

CHAPTER 6
MEATS AND STEWS

Brunswick Stew from the VMFA Arts Café

Serves 8.

8 ounces bacon, chopped

1 large yellow onion, peeled and diced

4 cups chicken stock

1 pound fresh or frozen corn kernels

1 pound fresh or frozen baby lima beans

2 (16-ounce) cans diced tomatoes

2 (16-ounce) cans tomato purée

1 pound pulled roasted chicken meat, dark and
   white meats combined

For the Roux

2 tablespoons unsalted butter

2 tablespoons all-purpose flour

1. In a large stock pot, sauté the bacon until slightly crisp. Remove the bacon with a slotted spoon and set aside.

2. Add the onion to the rendered bacon fat and sauté over medium heat until soft, about 10 minutes. Add the chicken stock and bring to a simmer. Add the corn and lima beans and simmer, uncovered, 5 minutes. Add the tomatoes and tomato purée, then return the bacon to the pot and simmer 10 minutes longer.

3. To prepare the roux, melt the butter in a small, heavy saucepan over medium heat. Add the flour, whisk until smooth, and continue cooking over medium-low heat until the roux is slightly browned, about 8 to 10 minutes. Whisk the roux into the simmering stew until it thickens slightly.

4. To finish the stew, add the chicken and heat through.

Danny Ayers, Executive Chef
VMFA, Richmond

Home-Style Stewed Chicken

Serves 4.

Very simple and very comforting

1 (3 to 4-pound) chicken, cut into 8 pieces

1 large onion, peeled and diced

3 stalks celery, diced

2 carrots, peeled and sliced

3 white potatoes, peeled and cut into $\frac{1}{2}$-inch slices

2 tomatoes (fresh or canned), cored, seeded, and
    diced

2 tablespoons minced fresh garlic (or substitute
    granulated garlic)

2 tablespoons dried basil

$\frac{1}{4}$ cup dry white wine

2 tablespoons ketchup

1 tablespoon paprika

1 teaspoon granulated sugar, or more to taste

Salt and freshly ground pepper to taste

4 to 6 cups hot cooked rice

1. Place the chicken in a large stock pot. Add the vegetables, garlic, basil, wine, ketchup, and paprika. Add enough water to just cover the chicken and vegetables.

2. Bring the pot to a simmer and cook over very low heat, partially covered and stirring occasionally, for $1\frac{1}{4}$ to $1\frac{1}{2}$ hours. Meanwhile, prepare the rice.

3. When the chicken is done, stir in the sugar and season to taste with salt and pepper. Serve over mounds of hot rice.

Jim Schuyler, Executive Director
Beth Ahabah Museum and Archives, Richmond

The Brand Family's "Orange" Chicken

Serves 6.

This dish has no oranges in it, but was named for its vivid color.

Serve over fluffy white rice, with a salad on the side.

1 (6-ounce) can tomato paste
1 teaspoon mild prepared mustard
1 tablespoon Worcestershire sauce
2 egg yolks
1 cup (8 ounces) plain yogurt
2 tablespoons olive oil
1 large onion, peeled and diced
2 cloves fresh garlic, minced
1 teaspoon minced fresh ginger root
2 pounds boneless, skinless chicken breasts, cut into
   1-inch-thick strips

1. In a small mixing bowl, whisk together the tomato paste, mustard, Worcestershire sauce, egg yolks, and yogurt. Set the mixture aside.

2. Heat the olive oil in a saucepan or skillet. Add the onion, garlic, and ginger and sauté until soft and golden, about 10 to 15 minutes. Add the chicken and sauté until evenly browned, about 10 minutes.

3. Add the reserved yogurt mixture and bring to a simmer. Lower heat and cook, uncovered, an additional 12 to 15 minutes. Serve over mounds of hot rice.

Tina Brand
VMFA, Richmond

Easy Chicken and Sausage Cassoulet

Serves 6.

From Barbara Parker's grandmother's recipe file—great served over white or brown steamed rice, accompanied by a crisp, green salad and French baguette.

3 slices of bacon, diced

6 boneless, skinless, chicken thighs

½ teaspoon salt

¼ teaspoon freshly ground pepper

1 cup chopped onion

2 teaspoons minced fresh garlic

½ cup dry white wine

1 (28-ounce) can diced tomatoes, drained

½ bay leaf

½ teaspoon dried thyme leaves

½ teaspoon dried rosemary leaves

1 (9-ounce) can cannellini beans, drained and rinsed

4 ounces kielbasa, or other precooked, link sausage

1. In a large covered skillet or Dutch oven, sauté the bacon until crisp, then remove it with a slotted spoon and set aside.

2. Season the chicken with the salt and pepper, then brown it evenly in the rendered bacon drippings, about 3 minutes per side. Remove the chicken from the pan and reserve.

3. Add the onion to the pan and sauté 5 minutes; add the garlic and sauté a minute more. Add the wine, tomatoes, bay leaf, thyme, and rosemary and stir. Return the chicken to the pot and bring to a boil. Reduce the heat and simmer, partially covered, for 20 minutes.

4. To finish the cassoulet, add the beans and sausage, return the reserved cooked bacon to the pot and simmer, uncovered, an additional 10 minutes, or until heated through.

Barbara Parker, Director of Programs
Piedmont Arts Association, Martinsville

Almond and Cranberry-Stuffed Turkey Cutlets with Herb Cream Sauce

Serves 4.

For the Stuffed Cutlets

4 (4 to 5-ounce) turkey breast cutlets, about $\frac{1}{2}$-inch-thick slices

$\frac{1}{2}$ French baguette, cut into $\frac{1}{2}$-inch cubes and dried overnight (about 3 cups)

8 ounces slivered almonds

6 ounces dried cranberries

$\frac{1}{2}$ teaspoon minced fresh thyme leaves

$\frac{1}{2}$ teaspoon minced fresh sage leaf

$\frac{1}{2}$ teaspoon minced fresh oregano leaves

1 teaspoon minced fresh garlic

$\frac{3}{4}$ to 1 cup chicken stock

For the Herb Cream Sauce

2 tablespoons butter

2 tablespoons all-purpose flour

2 cups chicken stock

$\frac{1}{4}$ cup heavy cream

$\frac{1}{2}$ teaspoon minced fresh thyme leaves

Salt and freshly ground pepper to taste

1. Preheat oven to 350°F. Combine the bread cubes, almonds, and cranberries in a large bowl. Add the thyme, sage, oregano, and garlic, and toss to combine. Slowly add the stock to the mixture while continuing to toss the ingredients together, until the bread cubes are just moistened—the stuffing should not be sticky or pasty.

2. Place the cutlets on a work surface, with narrow ends closest to you. Place $\frac{1}{4}$ of the stuffing mixture a short distance from the end of each cutlet. Roll the cutlet to wrap around the mound of stuffing and secure it with a toothpick or short bamboo skewer.

3. Place the cutlets in a roasting pan and cover with aluminum foil. Bake for approximately 45 minutes, until cooked through.

4. To prepare the Herb Cream Sauce, melt the butter in a heavy saucepan over medium heat. Add the flour and whisk until smooth. Add the chicken stock and whisk over medium heat until smooth and simmering. Cook, uncovered, 3 to 5 minutes.

5. Whisk in the cream, thyme, and salt and pepper to taste. Heat through. To serve, place a cutlet on each serving plate and spoon on a generous amount of sauce.

Danny Ayers, Executive Chef
VMFA, Richmond

"Arista" Roasted Pork Loin with Garlic and Rosemary

Serves 6 to 8.

Catherine Ritter gave this recipe to her VMFA colleagues and now, in Catherine's memory, we present it here. It's always a success. To quote Catherine, "I've often made two at a time, because everyone loves it, and if you are lucky, you may have some left over for sandwiches."

1 loin-end pork rib roast (5 to 7 pounds, bones split, or use a boneless roast)
3 tablespoons olive oil
10 large garlic cloves, slivered
2 tablespoons dried rosemary, crumbled
2 teaspoons coarse kosher salt
1 tablespoon coarsely ground black pepper
4 sprigs fresh rosemary

1. Preheat oven to 350°F. Cut $1/2$-inch-deep slits over the surface of roast. Be sure there are at least 3 slits per rib.

2. In a small bowl, combine the olive oil with the garlic, dried rosemary, salt, and pepper. Using the tip of a teaspoon or butter knife, stuff the slits in the pork roast with the garlic and herb mixture, then rub the remaining mixture over the surface of the roast.

3. Using a few lengths of kitchen twine, tie the sprigs of fresh rosemary to the roast. Place the roast, bone side down, in a sturdy, shallow roasting pan. Bake, uncovered, for 17 minutes per pound (about $1^1/2$ hours) or until the internal temperature reaches 165°F. The sliced roast can be served hot or at room temperature.

Anne Barriault, Writer-Editor
VMFA, Richmond

This is a lavish "Roman Style" roast, suitable for serving at Christmas and New Year's celebrations.

Clarke's Pork Chop Marinade

**Enough to cover 8 to 10
(4-ounce) chops.**

This marinade is also great
for marinating boneless,
skinless chicken breasts.

$1/4$ cup prepared teriyaki sauce

2 tablespoons brown sugar

2 teaspoons vegetable oil

$1/2$ teaspoon fresh ground black pepper

$1/4$ teaspoon seasoned salt, such as Lawry's brand
(optional)

1 clove fresh garlic, minced

2 teaspoons minced onion

2 teaspoons ground ginger

Whisk all the ingredients together and pour over
pork chops in a shallow glass pan. Cover with
plastic wrap and marinate in the refrigerator for 8 to
24 hours. The chops can then be char-grilled,
broiled, or pan-seared.

If using chicken, char-grill the breasts, then smother
them with grilled onions and melted cheese and
serve on buns.

**Beth Fox, Education Outreach Coordinator
Rawls Museum Arts, Courtland**

Hazelnut and Apple-Stuffed Pork Chops with Coffee Gravy

Serves 6.

Chef Bennett at The Jefferson Hotel in Richmond says, "If you can't find a good, rich demi-glace in your local gourmet food store, substitute rich brown gravy."

Garnish this dish with thin slices of apple and a few hazelnuts.

For the Stuffing

¼ cup (½ stick) butter

1 teaspoon ground cinnamon

1 apple, cored and finely chopped (Granny Smith or Cortland variety)

½ cup toasted hazelnuts, chopped

1 cup fresh bread crumbs, toasted

Salt and freshly ground pepper to taste

3 eggs, beaten

6 (5- to 6-ounce) thick-cut pork chops

½ cup clarified butter (see Recipe Note)

For the Gravy

½ cup dry white wine

¼ cup Applejack or apple brandy

2 teaspoons brown sugar, or more to taste

¼ cup (½ stick) cold butter, cut into pieces

½ cup demi-glace (reduced brown veal stock)

¼ cup brewed espresso coffee (or use regular brewed coffee for a milder flavor)

Thinly sliced apples and chopped hazelnuts for garnish

1. To prepare the stuffing, melt the butter in a large skillet over medium heat. Add the cinnamon and chopped apple and sauté for 2 minutes. Remove the pan from heat.

2. Add the hazelnuts and bread crumbs to the apple mixture and stir to combine. Allow the mixture to cool to room temperature, then season to taste with salt and pepper. Add the eggs and mix thoroughly.

3. Preheat the oven to 350°F. Cut a pocket in each pork chop and fill, using all the prepared stuffing.

4. Heat the clarified butter in a large, heavy skillet over medium-high heat. Brown the pork chops 2 or 3 at a time, for about 3 minutes per side. Lift the pork chops from the skillet and transfer them to a large, shallow roasting pan or casserole dish. Bake the pork chops for 15 to 20 minutes, until they are cooked through and the stuffing is warm.

5. While the pork chops are baking, prepare the gravy. Return the large skillet in which the pork chops were browned to high heat. Add the white wine to the remaining butter and pan juices and stir, scraping up any brown bits from the bottom of the

skillet. Reduce the heat to medium and simmer until the wine is reduced to 2 tablespoons.

6. Add the Applejack or brandy and brown sugar, taking care not to ignite the liquor. Allow the mixture to reduce by half. Whisk in the cold butter a piece at a time and heat it until it begins to foam. Add the demi-glace (or brown gravy) and brewed coffee.

7. Bring the mixture to a boil, whisking, and season to taste with salt, lots of black pepper, and additional brown sugar, if desired.

8. To serve, place the baked pork chops on a heated serving platter, drizzle the platter with the gravy, and garnish with apple slices and chopped hazelnuts.

Recipe Note
To make $1/3$ cup clarified butter, melt $1/2$ cup (1 stick) unsalted butter in a small saucepan. As the melted butter cools, the solids will go to the bottom. Carefully pour or spoon off the clarified, golden butter that rises to the top.

Jannequin Bennett, Chef
Greg Kernodle, Sous Chef
TJ's, The Jefferson Hotel, Richmond
Courtesy VMFA, Richmond

Marinated London Broil

Serves 4 to 6.

VMFA publications intern Rob Pretlow shared this recipe with colleagues when he was here. Says Anne Barriault, "I marinate it overnight, take it to the beach, and serve it for the first family vacation dinner."

"There are never any leftovers."

For the Marinade
$1/2$ cup soy sauce
$1/4$ cup vegetable oil
$1/2$ cup pineapple juice
1 clove fresh garlic, minced
1 tablespoon minced fresh ginger root
1 teaspoon lemon zest

1 to $1 1/2$-pound London Broil cut of beef

1. Whisk together all the marinade ingredients. Place the London Broil in a shallow glass pan or a zip-lock bag and pour on the marinade. Let the meat marinate for at least 8 hours, or up to 48 hours.

2. The meat is best char-grilled to medium-rare, then thinly sliced, crosswise, against the grain. It can also be broiled in the oven.

Anne Barriault, Writer-Editor
VMFA, Richmond

Roasted Rack of Summerfield Farm Spring Lamb with Stoneground Grits, Mint-Cherry Chutney, and Lamb "Gravy"

Serves 4.

This recipe calls for a "Frenched" rack of lamb, which is actually a rib roast of lamb with the sinew and fatty tissues pared completely off the extended rib bones, leaving just the tender round of rib-eye meat intact and on the bone. A skilled butcher should be able to provide you with a neatly Frenched rack of lamb upon request.

A note from Chefs Bundy and Fernandes at Lemaire Restaurant in Richmond's Jefferson Hotel:

"At Lemaire we strive to use only the freshest local ingredients. The lamb we use comes from Summerfield Farm in the hills of the Blue Ridge Mountains. Summerfield Farm uses a free-roaming technique to graze. The end product is a rosy-colored meat with a wonderfully gentle flavor.

"The combination of lamb and coarse-ground grits is tremendously Southern. We were able to find a company—Byrd Mill—in Ashland, that produces a true coarse stone-ground grit. It is essential to have such a great product. We slowly cook the grits in chicken stock, milk, and herbs. After a period of about four hours they reach the consistency that we want. We then fold in rich mascarpone cheese to finish.

"It is a wonderful thing to be in Virginia and have such great products to work with. We truly believe in our local farmers and their methods. Without their help, Lemaire wouldn't be the restaurant it is today."

First, prepare the grits and chutney. Be ready to plate the lamb shortly after it comes out of the oven, hot and fragrant.

For the Grits
1½ cups Byrd Mill Stoneground Grits
2 cups chicken stock
3 cups whole milk, or more as needed
¾ cup (1½ sticks) butter
½ cup mascarpone cheese
Salt and freshly ground white pepper to taste

1. Combine the grits, stock, milk, and butter in a 2-quart saucepan and bring to a simmer. Set the heat to the lowest possible setting and simmer the grits, uncovered, for approximately 4 hours, or until they are soft and creamy. Stir often to make sure the grits do not stick to the pan, and add more milk as needed to maintain a creamy consistency.

2. Just before you are ready to serve the finished dish, reheat the grits, stir in the Mascarpone cheese, and season with salt and white pepper to taste.

For the Mint-Cherry Chutney
1 cup dried cherries
5 ounces port

1 shallot, minced
1 tablespoon red wine vinegar
1 tablespoon granulated sugar
2 tablespoons thinly slivered fresh mint leaves

Place all ingredients—except the mint—in a small, non-reactive saucepan and bring to a simmer over low heat. Cook for approximately 25 to 30 minutes, or until the cherries are plump and softened. Remove the pan from the heat and fold in the mint. Set the chutney aside to cool.

For the Lamb
2 whole Frenched racks of lamb (10 to 12 ounces
   each, 8 ribs per rack)
1 teaspoon salt
$\frac{1}{2}$ teaspoon ground white pepper
1 cup whole grain mustard
$\frac{1}{2}$ cup good-quality bourbon
2 cups fine, fresh bread crumbs
$\frac{1}{3}$ cup clarified butter (see Recipe Note)

1. Preheat oven to 450°F. Season all sides of the lamb with the salt and white pepper. In a bowl, whisk together the bourbon and mustard until smooth. Thinly coat the lamb racks with the mixture on all sides, then dredge in fresh bread crumbs.

2. Heat the clarified butter in a large skillet or sauté pan. Evenly brown the lamb racks on all sides, turning, for about 2 to 3 minutes per side. When they are browned, transfer them to a shallow roasting pan and bake for approximately 18 to 20 minutes for medium-rare; ten minutes longer for medium to well-done.

3. Allow the lamb to rest on a carving platter for about 8 to 10 minutes before cutting into individual chops. Allow any warm carving juices, "gravy," to drain into the platter as you carve.

4. To serve, place a generous scoop of warm grits in the middle of each serving plate and arrange 4 chops around it. Drizzle with lamb gravy and garnish with a heaping spoonful of Mint-Cherry Chutney.

Recipe Note
To make $\frac{1}{3}$ cup clarified butter, melt $\frac{1}{2}$ cup (1 stick) unsalted butter in a small saucepan. As the melted butter cools, the solids will go to the bottom. Carefully pour or spoon off the clarified, golden butter that rises to the top.

You can contact Summerfield Farm in Culpeper at 1-800-898-3276 to order their special racks of spring lamb.

Walter Bundy, Executive Chef
Duane Fernandes, Sous Chef
Lemaire Restaurant
The Jefferson Hotel, Richmond
Courtesy VMFA, Richmond

Spiced Leg of Lamb
or "Mughlai Raan"

Serves 6 to 8.

This lamb is slow-roasted and is traditionally served well-done, but can be served rare or medium-rare, according to personal preference.

For the Marinade

2 large Spanish onions, peeled and quartered

4 cloves fresh garlic

2 tablespoons coarsely chopped fresh ginger root

1 tablespoon almonds

1 tablespoon raisins

2 teaspoons whole coriander seeds (or 1 teaspoon ground coriander)

2 teaspoons chili powder

1 teaspoon whole cumin seeds (or ½ teaspoon ground cumin)

4 whole cloves (or ½ teaspoon ground cloves)

2 teaspoons turmeric

2 teaspoons garam masala

Fresh-squeezed juice of 1 lemon

1 cup plain yogurt

2 tablespoons tomato paste

Salt to taste

1 (6 to 8-pound) leg of lamb, bone-in

1. Place the onions, garlic, ginger root, almonds, and raisins in a blender or the bowl of a food processor fitted with a steel blade. Pulse until the onions are coarsely chopped. Add all the remaining marinade ingredients and pulse to combine, until the onion is finely grated in texture.

2. Trim away the thick, fatty tissues and any "silver skin" from the surface of the roast. Rinse the lamb and pat dry with paper towels. With the tip of a sharp paring knife, cut deep slits into the meat, then rub the marinade over the entire roast, taking care to fill the slits. Cover with plastic wrap and refrigerate for at least 24 hours, and up to 48 hours.

3. Preheat oven to 325°F. Place the roast on a rack in a shallow roasting pan, pouring the marinade over the roast and into the pan. Bake 25 minutes per pound (about 2 hours) for medium doneness, basting every 15 to 20 minutes. For well-done lamb, bake to an internal temperature of 175°F.

4. Let the roast rest for 10 minutes before carving. Save the pan juices and serve in a gravy boat alongside the roast.

Tina Brand
VMFA, Richmond

CHAPTER 7

DESSERTS

Clevie Wingate's Pound Cake

Serves 8 to 10.

5 eggs

2 cups granulated sugar

3 cups all-purpose flour

1 cup whole milk

1 cup vegetable shortening (or substitute vegetable oil)

1 tablespoon baking powder

1/2 teaspoon salt

1 teaspoon vanilla

1 teaspoon lemon extract

1. Preheat oven to 350°F. Generously grease and flour a tube pan.

2. In a large mixing bowl, using an electric mixer, beat together the eggs and sugar until light, about 2 minutes. Fold in all the remaining ingredients and beat with a spatula until smooth.

3. Spoon the batter into the prepared tube pan and smooth the surface with a spatula. Bake 60 to 70 minutes, or until a toothpick inserted in the center comes out clean. Cool the cake in the pan for 10 to 15 minutes before inverting it onto a serving plate.

Clevie Wingate
Courtesy Blue Ridge Institute, Ferrum

Marmalade Polenta Cake

Serves 10 to 12.

1 cup self-rising flour

2/3 cup quick-cooking style polenta

2/3 cup ground almonds

5 ounces (1 stick, plus 1 tablespoon) chilled butter, cut into pieces

1 cup granulated sugar

2 eggs, lightly beaten

1/2 cup whole milk

1/2 cup orange marmalade

1. Preheat oven to 350°F. Butter an 8-inch round cake pan and line the bottom with a round of waxed or parchment paper.

2. Place the flour, polenta, almonds, butter, and sugar in the bowl of a food processor and pulse just until the mixture resembles fine bread crumbs. Add the eggs, milk, and marmalade and pulse to combine.

3. Spoon the batter into the cake pan and smooth the surface with a spatula. Bake 60 to 70 minutes, or until a toothpick inserted in the center comes out clean. Allow the cake to cool in the pan for 10 minutes, then invert onto a serving plate. Serve at room temperature.

Tina Brand
VMFA, Richmond

German Carrot Cake

Serves 10.

1½ cups granulated sugar

1½ cups vegetable oil

4 eggs

2 cups unbleached flour

2 teaspoons baking soda

2 teaspoons ground cloves

½ teaspoon ground nutmeg

2 teaspoons ground cinnamon

3 cups peeled, grated carrots

1 cup chopped pecans or walnuts

For the Frosting

4 ounces cream cheese at room temperature

3 tablespoons butter at room temperature

1½ cup powdered sugar

½ teaspoon vanilla

2 tablespoons apricot jam

1 cup finely chopped pecans or walnuts

1. Preheat oven to 350°F. Grease a 13x9x2-inch glass baking pan, or other large cake pan.

2. In a large mixing bowl, stir together the granulated sugar and vegetable oil. Using a spatula or wooden spoon, add the eggs one at a time, beating well after each addition.

3. In another bowl, sift together the flour, baking soda, cloves, nutmeg, and cinnamon. Add the dry ingredients by fourths to the egg mixture. Fold in the carrots and nuts.

4. Spoon the batter into the prepared baking pan and bake 40 to 45 minutes, or until the edges of the cake begin to pull away from the pan and a toothpick inserted in the center comes out clean. Remove the cake from the oven and cool completely, in the pan, before frosting.

5. To prepare the frosting, blend the cream cheese and butter together in a medium mixing bowl. Sift in the powdered sugar and beat with a spatula until smooth. Beat in the vanilla and apricot jam. Ice the top of the cake and cover with the nuts.

Dot Woodall, Painter, Studio #7
Torpedo Factory Arts Center, Alexandria

Three-Layer Banana Cake

Serves 8 to 10.

1½ cups (3 sticks) butter at room temperature

2 cups granulated sugar

2 eggs

3 cups all-purpose flour

2 teaspoons baking soda

1 cup whole milk

3 ripe bananas, peeled and mashed

For the Icing

8 ounces cream cheese at room temperature

1 pound powdered sugar

1 teaspoon vanilla

1 teaspoon whole milk, or more

1½ cups chopped pecans

1. Preheat oven to 350°F. Butter or grease three 9-inch round cake pans and line the bottoms with rounds of waxed or parchment paper.

2. In a large mixing bowl, beat the butter and granulated sugar until light and smooth, using an electric mixer or wooden spoon. Add the eggs one at a time, beating well after each addition.

3. In another bowl, sift together the flour and baking soda.

4. Gradually add the dry ingredients to the butter and egg mixture, alternating with the milk, until blended. Fold in the bananas. Spoon the batter into the prepared baking pans and bake about 30 minutes, or until a toothpick inserted in the centers comes out clean.

5. Cool the cake in the pans for 30 minutes, then invert them onto racks to cool completely.

6. To prepare the icing, beat together the cream cheese, powdered sugar, and vanilla until smooth. Add milk by teaspoons to reach the desired fluffy consistency. Ice the tops of each cake layer, sprinkle ½ cup chopped pecans on each, then stack them to form a three-layer cake.

Jacqueline S. Brownfield
University of Virginia Art Museum
Charlottesville

Passover Chocolate-Chip Sponge Cake

Serves 6 to 8.

10 eggs, separated
1½ cups granulated sugar, divided
¼ cup potato starch
½ cup matzo cake meal
1 cup mini chocolate chips

1. Preheat oven to 350°F. Lightly grease a 10-inch tube or springform cake pan.

2. In a large mixing bowl, beat the egg yolks until light using an electric mixer. Set aside 2 tablespoons of the sugar. Beat all the remaining sugar (1 cup, plus 6 tablespoons) into the egg yolks.

3. In another large mixing bowl, beat the whites with the reserved 2 tablespoons of sugar to form stiff peaks.

4. Slowly add the potato starch, then the matzo cake meal, to the egg-yolk mixture, beating with a spatula after each addition. Fold in the egg whites and combine well, then fold in the chocolate chips.

5. Pour the batter into the prepared cake pan and smooth the surface with a spatula. Bake for 50 to 55 minutes, or until a toothpick inserted in the center comes out clean. Allow the cake to cool in the pan briefly, about 15 minutes, then invert it onto a serving plate and cool one hour before serving.

Bonnie Eisenman, Administrative Assistant
Beth Ahabah Museum and Archives, Richmond

Blue Ridge Bread Pudding

Serves 6 to 8.

This recipe has been in Gail Holley's family for five generations.

Very comforting, especially accompanied by a scoop of vanilla ice cream.

1 egg, beaten
1 cup granulated sugar
1 teaspoon vanilla
2½ cups whole milk
¼ cup (½ stick) butter, cut into pieces
3 cups coarsely crumbled home-baked biscuits

1. Preheat oven to 425°F. Lightly grease or butter a 13x9x2-inch baking pan, or other ovenproof casserole.

2. Whisk together the egg, sugar, vanilla, and milk. Add the butter and crumbled biscuits and fold to combine. Pour the mixture into the baking pan and bake 40 to 45 minutes, gently stirring the pudding twice as it bakes, until it is set and lightly browned on top. Serve warm, or at room temperature.

Gail Holley
Courtesy Blue Ridge Institute, Ferrum

Coconut Tapioca Pudding

Serves 6.

This pudding can be served warm or chilled, in individual serving cups. Chef Frank garnishes the pudding with toasted coconut and almonds, diced fresh mango, or crystallized ginger.

3⅓ cups unsweetened coconut milk
⅔ cup small pearl tapioca
⅔ cup granulated sugar
1 vanilla bean pod, split
Pinch of salt

1. Combine all the ingredients in a heavy saucepan and bring to a simmer. Continue to simmer over very low heat, stirring constantly with a wooden spoon, for 10 to 12 minutes, or until the mixture is thick and creamy and the tapioca is tender.

2. Remove the pan from the heat and set aside to cool, about 30 to 45 minutes. Remove the vanilla bean from the pudding. Lay the pod on a flat work surface and, using a sharp paring knife, scrape the tiny seeds from inside the pod and return them to the pudding. Stir again to blend.

3. Spoon the pudding into 6 individual serving cups or wine glasses. For chilled pudding, cover with plastic wrap and refrigerate at least 3 hours before serving.

J. Frank, Personal Chef to Frances Lewis
Courtesy VMFA, Richmond

The Jefferson Hotel's Bananas Foster

Serves 8.

¼ cup (½ stick) butter
¼ cup brown sugar
4 bananas, peeled and sliced in half, lengthwise
1 cinnamon stick
Fresh-squeezed juice of 1 lemon
Fresh-squeezed juice of 1 orange
3 ounces banana liqueur
4 ounces Myer's dark rum
8 scoops French vanilla ice cream

1. Melt the butter and brown sugar in a skillet over medium heat for 2 minutes.

2. Add the bananas, cinnamon stick, juices, liqueur and rum, and sauté for 3 more minutes, gently turning the bananas to brown them lightly.

3. Remove the pan from heat and spoon a banana slice into each serving dish. Top with a scoop of ice cream, then drizzle on the warm pan liquids and serve.

The Jefferson Hotel, Richmond
Courtesy VMFA, Richmond

Jersey Dirt

Serves 12.

1 (6-serving size) box instant vanilla pudding
4 ounces cream cheese at room temperature
$\frac{1}{4}$ cup ($\frac{1}{2}$ stick) butter at room temperature
$\frac{1}{4}$ cup powdered sugar
1 cup prepared whipped dessert topping
   (or sweetened whipped cream)
1 teaspoon vanilla
8 ounces finely crumbled Oreo cookies

1. Prepare the vanilla pudding according to package directions, then transfer to a large mixing bowl and set aside to cool completely.

2. In a small mixing bowl, cream together the cream cheese, butter, and powdered sugar until smooth.

3. Fold the whipped dessert topping (or whipped cream) and the vanilla into the cooled pudding. Add the cream cheese and butter mixture and blend until smooth.

4. Lightly press half the crumbled cookies into a 13x9x2-inch glass baking pan. Spoon the pudding mixture over the cookies and smooth the surface with a spatula. Top evenly with the remaining crumbled cookies.

5. Cover with plastic wrap and chill at least 3 hours, until firm and set. To serve, cut into squares.

Former Student
University of Richmond

Raspberry Cream Cheese Pie

Serves 6.

4 ounces cream cheese at room temperature

$1/4$ cup powdered sugar

$1/2$ teaspoon vanilla

$41/4$ cups prepared whipped dessert topping
(or sweetened whipped cream), divided

1 10-inch pie shell, prebaked and cooled

4 cups fresh raspberries

1 cup granulated sugar

$1/4$ cup raspberry-flavored gelatin mix

$1/4$ cup cornstarch

1 cup water

1. In a large mixing bowl, cream together the cream cheese, powdered sugar, and vanilla until smooth. Fold in $21/4$ cups whipped dessert topping (or sweetened whipped cream). Spread the mixture in the prebaked pie shell. Cover and refrigerate for at least one hour.

2. Place the raspberries in a mixing bowl. In a saucepan, combine the granulated sugar, gelatin, cornstarch, and water. Bring to a boil and simmer 1 minute, stirring constantly. Pour the mixture over the raspberries and gently stir to combine. Allow the mixture to cool slightly, then spoon into the pie, covering the chilled cream mixture. Cover again with plastic wrap and chill overnight.

3. To serve, cover the pie with the remaining 2 cups whipped dessert topping (or sweetened whipped cream) and cut into wedges.

Mary Backels, Membership Chair
Alleghany Highlands Arts & Crafts Center
Clifton Forge

Chocolate-Cappuccino Pots Au Crème

Serves 6.

The best-quality, "couverture" dark chocolate makes the very best pots au crème, also called "pots de crème au chocolat." Chef Herndon uses imported dark chocolate with at least 73 percent cocoa butter content.

The pots au crème are baked in a water bath. To prepare the water bath, bring a large, full kettle of water to a boil. Place a roasting pan large enough to hold six 5-ounce ramekins or custard cups in the preheated oven, arrange the filled ramekins in the roasting pan, then pour in enough boiling water to reach half-way up the sides of the ramekins. Bake as directed, removing the roasting pan carefully when the pots au crème are done.

2 cups whole milk
1¼ cups granulated sugar
1 vanilla bean, slit in half lengthwise with center
    contents removed
8 ounces good-quality dark or bittersweet chocolate
2 tablespoons brewed espresso coffee
2 tablespoons cappuccino- or coffee-flavored
    liqueur
7 egg yolks
Sweet whipped cream, fresh raspberries, and mint
    sprigs for garnish

1. Preheat oven to 325°F. In a heavy saucepan, combine the milk, sugar, and vanilla bean. Bring to a gentle simmer and stir just until the sugar has dissolved. Remove from heat and strain the mixture through cheesecloth or very fine wire-mesh strainer. Return the mixture to the saucepan.

2. Add the chocolate and stir until it has melted, over very low heat if necessary—do not allow the mixture to boil. Remove the pan from the heat, stir in the espresso and liqueur, and set aside to cool slightly.

3. In a mixing bowl, whisk the egg yolks until light, then slowly whisk them into the chocolate mixture. Divide the mixture evenly among the ramekins or custard cups. Arrange the ramekins in a water bath, as directed above, and bake 30 to 40 minutes, until the pots au crème are set and firm.

4. Chill the ramekins before serving and garnish with dollops of whipped cream, fresh raspberries, and mint sprigs.

Mark Herndon, Executive Chef
The Governor's Executive Mansion, Richmond
Courtesy VMFA, Richmond

Peach Crème Brûlée with Blackberry-Sage Compote

Serves 10.

This recipe is baked in a water bath using the same method as described in the preceding recipe for "Chocolate-Cappuccino Pots Au Crème."

1 pound locally-grown ripe peaches, peeled, pitted, and coarsely chopped

$1/4$ cup peach schnapps

1 cup whole milk

3 cups heavy cream

1 vanilla bean, slit lengthwise

1 tablespoon peeled, grated fresh ginger root

1 cup granulated sugar, plus additional for caramelizing the crème brûlée

9 egg yolks

1. Preheat oven to 325°F. In a heavy saucepan, combine the peaches and schnapps and simmer over medium heat until the peaches are tender. Set aside and allow to cool slightly, then place the mixture in a blender or food processor and purée.

2. Return the purée to the saucepan and add the milk, cream, vanilla bean, ginger root, and half of the sugar, and bring to a boil, stirring.

3. In a large mixing bowl, whisk together the remaining sugar with the egg yolks until light.

Slowly whisk the heated peach and milk mixture into the eggs, then strain the mixture through a fine wire mesh sieve.

4. Divide the mixture among ten 6-ounce crème brûlée ramekins. Arrange the ramekins in a water bath and bake until set and firm, about 45 minutes. Allow them to cool in the water bath, then remove the ramekins, cover with plastic wrap and refrigerate overnight.

5. Evenly sprinkle the tops of the crème brûlée with a thin layer of sugar. Use a chef's blowtorch to melt and brown the sugar, or arrange the ramekins on a baking sheet and place under a very hot broiler for just a minute or two, watching constantly, until they are browned. To serve, top each ramekin with a generous spoonful of Blackberry-Sage Compote.

For the Blackberry-Sage Compote

$1/4$ cup Late Harvest Vidal or other fine-quality sweet dessert wine

1 tablespoon balsamic vinegar

$1/4$ cup granulated sugar

2 pints fresh blackberries

1 tablespoon finely chopped fresh sage

1. In a heavy saucepan, combine the wine, vinegar, and sugar and simmer over medium heat, stirring, until reduced by half.

2. Add the blackberries and continue cooking until they begin to soften. Remove the pan from the heat and stir in the sage. Cover and refrigerate until cold.

Mark W. Herndon, Executive Chef
The Governor's Executive Mansion, Richmond
Courtesy VMFA, Richmond

Million-Dollar Birthday Cookies

**Makes 2 dozen
4-inch cookies.**

3 ounces white chocolate, coarsely chopped

2 cups all-purpose flour

1 teaspoon baking soda

½ teaspoon salt

1 cup firmly packed light brown sugar

¾ cup (1½ sticks) unsalted butter, cut into pieces

½ cup granulated sugar

2 large eggs

1 large egg yolk

1½ cups pecans, toasted and coarsely chopped

8 ounces semisweet baking chocolate, chopped into
   ¼-inch pieces

1 teaspoon vanilla

1. Preheat oven to 350°F. In a small, heavy saucepan, melt the white chocolate over very low heat, stirring, then quickly remove the pan from the heat and set aside.

2. Sift the flour, baking soda, and salt together into a mixing bowl.

3. In another large mixing bowl, using an electric mixer set to low speed, cream together the brown sugar, butter, and granulated sugar. Scrape down the sides of the bowl with a spatula, then beat on high speed for about 5 minutes, or until the mixture is smooth.

4. Add the eggs one at a time, followed by the egg yolk, beating on medium speed for 30 seconds after each addition, while frequently scraping down the sides of the bowl.

5. Add the melted white chocolate and beat on medium speed for 1 minute. Set the mixer to low speed, then gradually add the sifted dry ingredients. With a spatula, fold in the pecans, chopped semisweet chocolate, and vanilla.

6. Line two baking sheets with wax or parchment paper, or other non-stick covering. Use a large serving spoon or medium-sized ice cream scoop filled with 3 generous tablespoons of dough to form each cookie. Drop the dough onto the baking sheets, leaving 4 inches between each cookie. Bake 18 to 20 minutes, rotating the baking sheets 180 degrees after the first 10 minutes.

7. Remove the cookies from the oven and cool to room temperature on the baking sheets, about 30 minutes. Store the cookies in a tightly sealed plastic container.

**Marcel Desaulniers, Chef/Owner
The Trellis, Williamsburg
Courtesy VMFA, Richmond**

PARTICIPANTS, WORKS OF ART, AND INDEX

PARTICIPATING
ORGANIZATIONS

Alleghany Highlands Arts & Crafts Center,
    Clifton Forge
Artisans Center of Virginia, Waynesboro
Beth Ahabah Museum and Archives, Richmond
Blue Ridge Institute, Ferrum College
Chrysler Museum of Art, Norfolk
Danville Museum of Fine Arts and History
Daura Gallery, Lynchburg College
Hampton University Museum,
    Hampton University
Hollins Art Gallery, Hollins University, Roanoke
McLean Project for the Arts
Peninsula Fine Arts Center, Newport News
Piedmont Arts Association, Martinsville
Radford University Art Museum
Rawls Museum Arts, Courtland
Thomas Jefferson Memorial Foundation,
    Charlottesville
Torpedo Factory Art Center, Alexandria
University of Richmond Museums
University of Virginia Art Museum, Charlottesville
Virginia Museum of Fine Arts, Richmond
Virginia Tech, Blacksburg
Virginia's Explore Park, Roanoke
William King Regional Arts Center, Abingdon

WORKS OF ART

Six Wine Glasses, c. 1900
Attributed to Glasfabrik Ludwig
Moser & Sohne, founded 1857,
Karlovy Vary Karlsbad, Western
Bohemia Region, Czech Republic
Crystal with hand-painted gilt
enamel
14/Y 1. Clear bowl with lavender petals; green and orange petals
 at stem base
14/V 2. Clear bowl with orange petals around bowl; four orange
 petals at stem base
14/R 3. Purplish bowl with blue petals; five orange and yellow
 petals at stem base
14/Z 4. Purplish bowl with four blue petals; six green petals at
 stem base
14/ZZ 5. Green bowl with purple ruffled petals; three purple
petals at stem base
14/N 6. Green bowl with orange tipped petals; four orange tipped
 petals at stem base
Each 7 1/16 x 2 5/8 inches
VMFA. Gift of Collen Wade, 2002.560.1-6

Susan Eder (American)
Popcorn Faces, 1986
Color photograph mounted on
matboard
30 x 28 inches
Joel and Lila Harnett Museum of
Art, University of Richmond
Museums, Gift of the Artist ©
Susan Eder

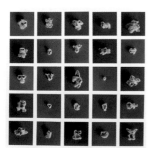

Jan Davidsz de Heem (Dutch)
Still Life, ca. 1640-50
Oil on canvas
32 x 42 inches
Virginia Museum of Fine Arts.
The Arthur and Margaret Glasgow
Fund, 61.15

Jan Miense Molenaer (Dutch)
An Allegory of Marital Fidelty,
1633
Oil on canvas
39 x 55½ inches
VMFA. The Adolph D. and
Wilkins C. Williams Collection,
49.11.19

Inkwell, c. 1906-12
Tiffany Studios (New York, 1900-
1938)
Bronze, oyster shell
3½ x 7½ x 7½ inches
VMFA. Gift of Sydney and Frances
Lewis, 85.84

One of a Pair of Champagne Flutes
Fabergé firm (Russian, St. Petersburg,
1896-1903)
Mikhail Perkhin, Workmaster (1860-
1903)
Glass, red and green gold
7³/₈ x 2¹³/₃₂ inches
VMFA. Bequest of Lelia Blair
Northrop, 78.78.¹/₂

Francois Boucher (French)
Pastorale: The Vegetable Vendor, ca. 1735
Oil on canvas
95 x 67 inches
Chrysler Museum of Art, Norfolk,
Virginia, Gift of Walter P. Chrysler,
Jr., 71.504

Richard Diebenkorn (American)
Coffee, 1956
Oil on canvas
67 x 58³/₄ inches
Chrysler Museum of Art, Norfolk,
Virginia
Gift of Walter P. Chrysler, Jr.,
Courtesy of the Estate of Richard
Diebenkorn and Artemis Greenberg
Van Doren Gallery, New York,
71.2003

*Royal Tea Service, Déjeuner
Mosaïque Florentine*, 1814
Manufacture Nationale de
Sèvres (active 1756-present)
Cameo on tray painted by
Antoine Beranger (1785-1867).
Other pieces painted by Pierre
Huard (d. 1857).
Hard paste porcelain
.2a/b   Teapot: 7¹/₄ x 7¹/₂ x 4¹/₂ inches
         Cover: 1 x 2¹/₄ inches
.3   Milk Jug: 8¹/₄ x 3³/₄ inches
.4a/b   Sugar Bowl with cover: 4¹/₄ x 5³/₄ x 4 inches
.5a/b   Cup: 3 x 4¹/₂ x 2⁷/₈ inches
         Saucer: 1 x 6¹/₈ inches
.6a/b   Cup: 3 x 4¹/₂ x 2⁷/₈ inches
         Saucer: 1 x 6¹/₈ inches
VMFA. Gift of The Council of the Virginia Museum of Fine Arts,
in celebration of their 40th Anniversary, 94.58.2-6a/b

Harold Little (American)
Greengrocer, 1975
Etching
10¹¹/₁₆ x 5 inches
Radford University Art Museum,
Radford, Virginia 98.068

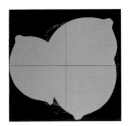

Donald Sultan (American)
Lemons, 1984
Latex, tar on vinyl tile over wood
97 x 97¹/₂ inches
VMFA. Gift of The Sydney and
Frances Lewis Foundation, 85.583

Sondra Freckelton (American)
Winter Melon with Quilt and Basket,
1977
Watercolor on paper
46¹/₈ x 44¹/₁₆ inches
VMFA. Gift of Sydney and Frances
Lewis, 85.388

Woman Bearing a Stemmed Cup
Mankot, 1700-10
Opaque watercolor on paper
7⁵/₈ x 4¹/₁₆ inches
VMFA. The Nasli and Alice
Heeramaneck Collection, Gift of
Paul Mellon, 68.8.93

Faith Ringgold (American)
Tar Beach II, 1990
Acid dyes screen printed on bleached
silk, and pieced, commercially
printed cotton
66 x 67¹/₂ inches
VMFA. Gift of Marion Boulton
Stroud, 2001.252

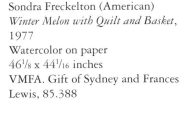

Richard La Barre Goodwin
(American)
Hunter's Cabin Door, ca. 1895
Oil on canvas
60¹/₂ x 36¹/₄ inches
VMFA. The Adolph D. and
Wilkins C. Williams Fund, 77.26

Alfred Sisley (French)
Fish on a Plate, 1865-67
Oil on canvas
18 x 22 inches
VMFA. Collection of Mr. and Mrs.
Paul Mellon, 83.50

Lewis Wickes Hine (American)
Oyster Shuckers, 1911
Photograph
4$\frac{1}{2}$ x 6$\frac{7}{8}$ inches
VMFA. Gift of Betty Stuart
Goldsmith Halberstadt and
Jon Halberstadt, 2003.121

Paul Gauguin (French)
Still Life with Oysters, 1876
Oil on canvas
21 x 36$\frac{3}{4}$ inches
VMFA. Collection of Mr. and
Mrs. Paul Mellon, 83.23

William Merritt Chase (American)
Still Life with Fish, ca. 1910
Oil on canvas
28$\frac{1}{2}$ x 41$\frac{1}{2}$ inches
VMFA. Gift of Mr. and Mrs. John
McGuigan and Museum Purchase,
The J. Harwood and Louise B.
Cochrane Fund for American Art,
2000.84

Statuette of Fish with Crown of Isis
Egyptian, ca. 1350 B.C.
Bronze with glass eyes
5$\frac{1}{8}$ x 7 x 2 inches
VMFA. Gift of Evelyn Maddox Pope
in memory of her husband Edward J.
Pope, 2001.247

Royal Linguist's Staff
Akan Culture, Asante Kingdom
(Ghana) 20th century
Wood, gold leaf
65$\frac{1}{2}$ x 7 x 8$\frac{1}{2}$ inches
VMFA. The Kathleen Boone Samuels
Memorial Fund, 86.200a/c.

Cornelis Jacobsz Van Delff
(Dutch)
Interior of a Kitchen, ca.1610s
Oil on canvas
45 x 75 inches
VMFA. Gift of Miss Ellen D.C.
Blair, 35.2.1

Etienne-Prosper Berne-Bellecour
(French)
La Desserte (The Remains of the
Meal), 1876
Oil on canvas
51 x 76$\frac{1}{2}$ inches
Chrysler Museum of Art, Norfolk,
Virginia, Museum Purchase with
funds from the Accessions Fund, Sheldon L. Breitbart Fund,
Walter P. Chrysler, Jr. Art Purchase Fund, and Grover Cleveland
Outland Memorial Fund, 2000.24

Berenice Abbott (American)
Zito Bakery, 1937
Silver print
9$\frac{5}{8}$ x 7$\frac{5}{8}$ inches
VMFA. The Adolph D. and
Wilkins C. Williams Fund, 75.48.4

Ewer
Japanese, 14th century
Negoro lacquer
12$\frac{1}{2}$ x 15$\frac{1}{4}$ x 10$\frac{1}{4}$ inches
VMFA. The Arthur and Margaret
Glasgow Fund, 73.41.a/b

INDEX